# Top Tips and Traps

**TIP**

There's a buyer for every home. The only real question is: How long will it take that person to find yours? (Chapter 1)

**TIP**

For most buyers, the perception is more important than the reality, the sizzle more mouthwatering than the steak. As long as buyers perceive your home to be desirable, it doesn't matter how bad a wreck it really is! (Chapter 1)

**TIP**

Anytime a buyer sees "seller financing" advertised or in a listing, it's a come-on. Immediately the buyer is more inclined to look at the property and to find a way to make an offer. (Chapter 1)

**TIP**

If you want to learn prices, become a "pretend" buyer for a weekend to quickly gain insights into the housing market in your area. (Chapter 4)

**TIP**

Good agents don't get rich by charging higher commissions or by browbeating sellers. They get rich by making more deals. (Chapter 5)

## TRAP

Just because the commission is negotiable is not necessarily a good reason to insist on a lower rate. Sometimes it's better to pay more to get better and quicker service. (Chapter 5)

## TRAP

Beware of the agent who insists on a very long listing. Giving a longer listing just might mean it will take longer to sell your house. (Chapter 5)

## TRAP

Do needed repair and cleanup work before listing; otherwise, buyers will characterize your property as a fixer-upper and will submit only lowball offers. (Chapter 8)

## TRAP

If you agree to finance the sale of your home creatively in order to make a deal, you could end up with a deal that would have been better not made. (Chapter 10)

## TIP

If you're willing to accept the buyer's price, you can often cut a deal with terms so favorable to you that it's better than getting your price! (Chapter 19)

## TIP

The longer you have your home on the market, the more you'll have to drop your price to attract buyers. Do what's necessary for a quick sale. (Chapter 19)

# Tips and Traps
# When Selling
# a Home

## Other McGraw-Hill Books by Robert Irwin

Tips and Traps When Buying a Home, Second Edition

Tips and Traps When Mortgage Hunting

Tips and Traps for Making Money in Real Estate

Buy, Rent, & Hold: How to Make Money in a "Cold" Real Estate Market

How to Find Hidden Real Estate Bargains, Revised First Edition

The McGraw-Hill Real Estate Handbook, Second Edition

Tips and Traps When Negotiating Real Estate

# Tips and Traps When Selling a Home

Robert Irwin

**Second Edition**

**McGraw-Hill**

New York  San Francisco  Washington, D.C.  Auckland  Bogotá
Caracas  Lisbon  London  Madrid  Mexico City  Milan
Montreal  New Delhi  San Juan  Singapore
Sydney  Tokyo  Toronto

**Library of Congress Cataloging-in-Publication Data**

Irwin, Robert.
    Tips and traps when selling a home / Robert Irwin.—2nd. ed.
       p.     cm.
    Includes index.
    ISBN 0-07-032885-4
    1. House selling.  2. Real estate business.  Title.
HD1379.I674     1996
333.33'83—dc20                      96-9177
                                                    CIP

# McGraw-Hill

*A Division of The McGraw·Hill Companies*

  2 3 4 5 6 7 8 9 0  DOC/DOC  9 0 1 0 9 8 7

ISBN 0-07-032885-4

*The sponsoring editor for this book was David Conti, the editing supervisor was Patricia V. Amoroso, and the production supervisor was Suzanne W. B. Rapcavage. It was set in Baskerville by Estelita F. Green of McGraw-Hill's Professional Book Group composition unit.*

*Printed and bound by R. R. Donnelley & Sons Company.*

This book is printed on recycled, acid-free paper containing a minimum of 50% recycled, de-inked fiber.

# Contents

# Preface

Selling your home shouldn't take a long time.

The longest it's taken me is about a month and usually it takes me only a week or less. That's not because I'm a great salesperson or because I'm especially lucky. I don't believe I have either of those attributes. Rather, it's because I find out what buyers are looking for and I make sure the home I'm selling fits their bill.

You can do the same thing.

My goal in writing this book is to present to you, the home seller (house, condo, co-op, or other property owner) a quick method of successfully selling your home. This book is filled with what I've discovered in 30 years of experience selling properties and learned from working with some of the best agents in the country. This book will give you tips to make your sale go quicker and easier, and it will alert you to the pitfalls and traps to avoid.

Finding a buyer for your home should not be frustrating, time-consuming, or emotionally and financially draining. It should be a pleasurable and profitable experience. My hope is that the second edition (completely updated and rewritten) of this best-selling book will be a clear and easy path showing you the way to…"sold!"

*Robert Irwin*

# Tips and Traps
# When Selling
# a Home

# 1

# Keys to Getting a Quick Sale

It can take a long time to make the decision to sell your home. But once you've decided, you'll probably want to sell immediately, tomorrow if not today. The last thing most people want is the nightmare of having a house up for sale month after month with no buyers. The cost, the lookers, the forever keeping it clean—you know the picture.

What's important to realize is that while most sellers take a fairly long time to sell, even in a strong market, some few are able to get rid of their homes almost overnight, even in a terrible market. What's the critical difference? What do those fast home sellers know that everyone else doesn't?

That's what we'll look at in this chapter. If you want to sell your home and want to do it quickly, you'll find the keys to doing it, here.

## What Attracts Buyers?

We all know that bees are attracted to sweets, cats like fish, dogs like bones—but what do home buyers like? What will induce them to get in their car and drive, sometimes long distances, to see your home? More important, what will get them to make an offer you'll like?

Here are the inducements in their usual order of importance. (Some buyers will be more interested in price, others in terms, but generally this is the pecking order.)

1. Neighborhood
2. Price
3. Appearance
4. Terms
5. Availability

You want to sell your home, today? Be sure that it's in a great neighborhood at a low price, that it shows well, that you offer easy-to-buy terms, and that you'll move out anytime the buyer wants to move in. It's sold, now!

Yeah, right...

Of course not. As sellers, how can we offer buyers everything they want? We can't move our house to a better neighborhood. We have a price we want and probably need to get. We can't change a one-story ranch into a two-story colonial. We probably can't give the seller a mortgage. And we need a place to move to before we can move out.

In other words, if you're the typical seller, you can find a lot of perfectly good reasons why you simply cannot offer buyers any of the five inducements noted above.

## What Does "Selling" a House Really Mean?

Which brings us to what selling a house actually involves. Most people simply call up a broker, list their property, and wait for the check to roll in. They want selling to be effortless and profitable.

But the broker isn't a magician and can't transform base metal into gold. He or she can only put the best face on what you have to offer (in terms of the five items just noted). If you're not offering much in the way of inducements, that's going to be a sour face no matter how good your agent is.

All of which is to say that "selling" your house is first up to you. It's your job to make your property highly salable. It's the sort of thing that experienced salespeople learn early on in their profession: A good product will sell itself. A bad product is a tough sell.

So what can you do to make your house more desirable to buyers? Let's consider each of the inducements that attract buyers and see if you can work with them.

## How Can I Improve the Neighborhood?

Obviously, you can't move your house to a better neighborhood. But you can do some things to improve the immediate neighborhood around you. And you can sometimes expand a potential buyer's perspective on the true quality of your area.

A few years ago a friend of mine had a home he was trying to sell in a rather rundown area. To make things worse, neighbors across the street were in the habit of dumping garbage on their own front lawn. Potential buyers would drive up to my friend's house, only to see the mess across the street. Most wouldn't even stop; they'd just drive on.

After nearly 15 months, my friend sold his property for far less than he had in it. He virtually "gave it away."

The new owner was an investor. She immediately put the house back up for sale. Then she went across the street to the bad neighbors, knocked on the door, and asked a favor. She said, "I'm trying to teach my son responsibility and how to do a good job. I wonder if you'd mind if he came over and mowed your lawn? It'll be a good experience for him."

The neighbor was astonished and looked across the street to a perfectly manicured lawn. "Sure," the neighbor said. "Why not?"

The new owner immediately sent her son over and in an afternoon the garbage-strewn lawn was clean as a whistle. The son even planted some flowers and washed off the driveway. She had her son do it a second time. Others in the neighborhood, who were relieved to see the mess cleaned up, began complimenting the bad neighbor, who got the idea. After that, although the lawn was never perfect, it was always mowed and there was no more garbage on it.

She resold that home within a few months for a substantial profit.

### TIP

When you can't move to a better neighborhood, try to improve the neighborhood you're in.

### Improve the Perception of the Neighborhood

Even if you do improve the look of homes on your street, you can't give your home a Beverly Hills address unless it's in Beverly Hills— or can you?

I once had a home that was in a modest area, but near the border of a highly desired area. When I advertised my property, did I say I was in the modest area? Or did my ad say "next to" the more desired neighborhood?

Further, when potential buyers stop by and are wary of the area, you can make an effort to demonstrate that your neighborhood is greatly underrated. You can point out that few people realize that you have a park nearby, are close to shopping, have great access to freeways, have green belts, or that your school tests scores are way up, or whatever. In other words, your neighborhood actually is far better than commonly perceived.

Further, you can explain that people are just now discovering the true value of your neighborhood. Why, within a year or two, yours could be among the most desired in the county, perhaps the state. The purchaser of your home will be getting in cheap, before people in general realize how much more desirable an area it really is and prices go up.

Will buyers believe it? If it's close enough to the truth, many will.

**TIP**

For most people the perception is more important than the reality, the sizzle more mouthwatering than the steak. As long as buyers perceive you're in a desirable neighborhood, it doesn't matter how good or bad your area really is.

## How Can I Get My Price, and Offer a Good Value to the Buyer Too?

You don't have to give the buyer a good price to sell your home. You just have to offer a realistic price.

The hardest thing for most sellers to accept is price realism. When you're selling, whether it be T-shirts, bananas, or houses, you're in competition with others selling the same or very similar products. If the vendor down the road is selling bananas for 67 cents a pound, how many people do you think will pay you $1.02 a pound? They'll say, "Why should I pay more? I'll go down the street and get the same bananas for less." It's the same for houses.

In order to sell, your price must be competitive. If you ask more than the market will bear, even just a few thousand dollars more, it'll take much longer to sell even in a strong market and you might never sell in a slow market.

### TRAP

If you want to sell, don't get hung up on "your price." A property is worth just what a buyer will pay for it, and no more. The hard truth is that it makes no difference how much you paid, how much you owe, or how much you put into it. Only the market determines the price.

### Getting a Better Price

With this said, it's important to understand that you can indeed get a better price than your neighbor for your house *if* you can convince a buyer that you have a superior product. The reason that you're charging $1.02 for your bananas is that they are organically grown. Or they are bigger. Or they taste better. Some buyers looking for a superior product will pay your higher price.

In other words, if you can convince buyers that your house is in some way superior to seemingly comparable homes selling for less, you can get more. The difficulty is in convincing the buyers, who these days are very savvy. Remember, buyers shop neighborhood first. Thus, they already have a good idea of what your house should be worth, given its location, even before they stop by.

Nevertheless, within every neighborhood there's a price *range*. You want to be at top of the range, not at the bottom or even near the middle. What can you do to accomplish this?

You can't change the size of your house. If you have 1500 square feet, you can't make it into 1800. (Unless you add on, but that might mean you're overbuilding for your neighborhood and you might get only 50 cents on the dollar for what it costs to do the work.) And you can't move your home to a better locale.

But you can "doll up" your house. You can make its appearance so irresistible that a buyer will perceive you have a better product and be willing to pay more for your home than for the "dog" that your neighbor down the street is selling for less.

## How Can I Improve My Home's Appearance?

There's an enormous amount you can do and we'll go into details in Chapter 8. But for now, let's assume that there's nothing drastically wrong with your home (no holes in the walls, no broken floors, no caved-in roof, and so on). Here are the four most important, inexpensive, and quick cosmetic improvements you can make.

### 1. Fix that driveway.

A driveway takes up an enormous amount of the front of your home. It's what people usually first see when they drive up. It's often what they first walk on. If it's cracked, broken, or even dirty, it sets the tone for the rest of the house.

Wash your driveway. (Use one of the many commercial cleaners available to get rid of stains.) If it's badly cracked and it's tar, have it resurfaced. It costs only a few hundred dollars. If the driveway is cement and it's cracked, have the cracked area cut out and replaced. Often you can replace a few sections for a fraction of what it will cost for an entirely new cement driveway.

### 2. Manicure the lawn and shrubs.

Again, first impressions are critical. You want the lawn to look like a carpet, the shrubs not to have a branch out of place. Get lots of green showing, water heavily for a month or more before you put the place up for sale, plant flowers—you get the idea.

### 3. Paint the front.

No, it's not expensive to paint the front of your house. It's expensive to paint your whole house, but not just the front. Most people can do it themselves. Use high-quality paint and a complementary color on the trim.

Most important, repaint that front door. The first physical contact a potential buyer makes with your house is the front door. (Why not pop for $50 and put on a new front door handle?)

### 4. Get rid of most of your furniture.

Yes, you want to paint and clean inside, and we'll have more to say about that later. But the biggest inside mistake that most sellers make is to confuse a "lived in" look with a selling look.

Buyers like spaciousness. They want to be able to imagine how their furniture will look in your home. Never mind that once they move in, it will be just as cluttered as your home is for you. You have to give them every opportunity to help them "see" themselves in your house.

Think of models for new homes that you may have seen. Did you notice that in the most charming models, the furniture was sparse, barely enough to live in, probably less than you'd find in the average hotel room?

You want to create an atmosphere of "negative space," where the rooms in your house cry out to be filled with more furniture, the buyer's furniture!

It doesn't matter what you do with most of your own furniture—put it in storage, leave it at a relative's or friend's house, store it, burn it! Just get rid of it to help sell your home.

## Should I Offer Better Terms to the Buyer?

What we all want is a buyer to come in and give us our price, *cash*.

The trouble is that these days, few buyers have cash. Indeed, according to government statistics, we're a nation of consumers, not savers. Exclusive of retirement, less than 30 percent of the population has any sizable amount of cash savings at all, certainly not enough to cover the down payment and closing costs when it comes time to buy a home.

Therefore, you can significantly increase the number of potential buyers for your home by offering to help them with the financing.

**TIP**

Anytime a buyer sees "seller financing" advertised or in a listing, it's a come-on. Immediately the buyer is more inclined to look at the property and to find a way to make an offer.

What is seller financing? Usually it means that you trade cash for paper. Instead of getting all cash back yourself, you carry back a second mortgage, usually for 10 percent or more of the selling price.

The second offers you pluses and minuses. On the upside, it brings you in cash each month, it's usually for a higher-than-market interest rate, and there's often a balloon payment after a few years. On the downside, you don't get all cash, which you may need in order to make another purchase of your own. And there's always the chance that the buyer might default somewhere down the road, meaning you might not get your money (or you might have to foreclose on the property). We'll discuss seller financing in detail in Chapter 10.

You want to sell faster and for more money? Offer the buyer financing. It makes your house much more desirable than those of other sellers who can't or won't.

## Should I Be Ready to Move on a Moment's Notice?

Sure, why not? After you sell you plan to move out anyway, don't you? So, if buyers come along who say that they'll take your place and close escrow in 3 weeks, provided you can move out by then, do it! You can always temporarily store your furniture and move into an apartment. But the important thing is that your house will be sold.

On the other hand, some buyers want a long escrow. They may not want to take possession until 90 or 120 days or more. They're waiting for their own home to close or for money to arrive from an inheritance, or have some other good reason for a delay. The point is, they want you to wait.

Should you? Certainly. If the buyers are qualified for financing and make a noncontingent offer (won't back out), and if they put up a big deposit, go for it. Of course, it's not a guaranteed sale, but it looks pretty good. And if you're worried, you can always insist that you be allowed to continue showing the property and accept backup offers from other buyers.

**TRAP**

My father, who worked in real estate for more than 35 years, used to say that he never felt sure a property was sold until he received the check in his hand—and even then he still wasn't completely sure! After 30 years in the field myself, I know just what he meant. There are no guaranteed sales, but sometimes you just have to take a chance on deals that look promising.

## The Keys to Quick Sales

As noted at the beginning of this chapter, if you're fortunate enough to be able to offer buyers all five key inducements, you'll have your house sold almost before the sign gets put up. They bear repeating:

1. Neighborhood
2. Price
3. Appearance
4. Terms
5. Availability

However, even if you can't offer all five, offer four, or three, or two. What's important is that you give the buyer *at least one good reason* to purchase your property over someone else's. We live in a highly competitive society, and nowhere is that competition tougher than in real estate. If you want to get your house sold, you need an edge. That edge comes from going out of your way to make your property salable.

**TIP**

There's a buyer for every house. The only real question is, how long will it take that person to find your property?

# 2

# Six Things to Do When You're Upside Down

*Upside down* is a term that sellers in a falling market have come to dread. It means that you owe more than your home is worth. If you sell at market, not only will you not receive any money back, you might have to put money into the deal out of your pocket just to make the sale! Consequently, even though you may need to, financially you can't sell. A great many sellers found themselves in just this predicament during the real estate recession of the early 1990s. Many are still in the same predicament today for one reason or another.

If you're upside down and you must sell because of job loss, transfer, illness, or other reason and you're sweating it, take heart. You should get some immediately useful answers in this chapter. If you're right side up, on the other hand, you may want to read on here, to see just how lucky you really are.

Here are six things to do when you're upside down.

## 1. Talk to Your Lender Immediately, Today, Right Now!

It's like meeting two bullies in an alleyway who look like they want to fight. You can "put up your dukes!" or you can see if you can talk your way out of it.

It's good advice.

**TIP**

 Talking to your adversary, whether a bully or a lender (some people would say there's not much difference!) transforms you from an object into a person. You've got a personality, you've got warmth, humor, and value. In short, it's a lot harder to beat up on someone you know and like than on a complete stranger.

As soon as you realize you're in trouble, contact your lender. "In trouble" means that you can't maintain the status quo. You've lost your job, you must move to keep your job, you're getting a divorce and the house must be sold, somebody's sick and you have to move, or something similar has happened. What it comes down to is that you've got to get out, but you owe more than your house is worth.

Contacting your lender, however, can be more difficult than it at first seems. After all, most lenders are giant institutions. How do you find the one person among hundreds of employees, perhaps thousands, who will respond to your needs?

Turn it around. If you don't contact your lender, and you stop making your mortgage payments, your lender will contact you. And the person making that contact may not be nearly as pleasant as the person you'll find if you go looking yourself.

## To Whom Do I Talk?

Often the best place to start is a local branch office, if your lender is a bank or savings and loan. If you know the employees there, they often can direct you to the right person. If not, you can always call your lender and simply start explaining your story. You may have to go through several at least partial explanations to get through to someone who will listen, understand, and, if not commiserate, at least take notes for future reference.

## What Do I Say?

In essence, what you tell your lender is that your home is not worth the mortgage amount and that you're having trouble making payments.

**TIP**

If you're up to date on your payments, most lenders don't want to talk to you. You're not a problem, yet. Until you're at least several months behind in payments, many lenders won't seriously deal with you.

Once you're several months behind, however, most lenders with whom you talk today will try to help you in several ways. They may be willing to allow you to miss payments for a period of time, if it appears you will be able to start making them again later on. (You're temporarily sick, for example.) Or they may restructure your loan, giving you lower payments. Or they might forgo interest for a period of time. Since the real estate recession of the early 1990s, most lenders have become quite adept at helping out troubled borrowers.

**TRAP**

Not all lenders are willing or able to help. You may just end up with a hardball lender that says simply, "Pay as agreed, or we'll foreclose." If that's the case, then you need to play hardball in return and say, "If you foreclose, you'll lose money. Let's work together on a better solution."

## 2. Consider a "Deed in Lieu of Foreclosure"

One possible solution is to deed the property directly to the lender. The lender can then attempt to resell it. Yes, you won't get anything out of this deal, but it helps protect your credit and gives you an honorable way out. Besides, by now you have no equity anyhow.

Why would a lender accept this option? Most don't, unless you make it more attractive to them. One person I know, after not making payments for 3 months and being threatened with foreclosure, called his lender and explained it this way: "If you accept a deed to the property in lieu of foreclosing, I'll be out next week and you'll get the house back in good shape, ready to resell.

"If, however, you refuse, then I'll sit in the house, without making payments, for the 5 months it takes to foreclose in this state. During that time anything can happen—the hardwood floors might get ruined, holes might get put in the walls, windows, sinks, and toilets could get broken. Neighborhood gangs might even come in and tear up and graffiti the place. You'll get it back after foreclosure, okay, but you may not like it!"

The lender agreed immediately to accept a deed in lieu of foreclosure. The seller played hardball.

### TRAP

 Lenders are aware of this ploy, and may go to court to get a restraining order against your damaging the property. The order, however, can be hard to enforce, particularly if you abandon the property and damage occurs from vandalism after you leave and before the lender gets possession. Also, you're responsible for keeping up the property as part of your loan agreement.

## 3. Negotiate a "Short Sale"

A short sale is a different tack. You suggest to the lender that the best way for both of you to get out of this predicament is for you to remain in the property, keeping it in good shape and finding a buyer. But because the house is worth less than the mortgage, you'll have to sell it for less. In other words, in order for you to make the sales effort, the lender will have to agree to take less—a short sale.

Will lenders agree?

Probably not, at least not formally. What many savvy lenders will say is something such as, "Keep trying to find a buyer who will pay off the entire mortgage. But if you can't and you do find a buyer in a short sale, we'll talk."

That's about the extent of a commitment to a short sale you're likely to get from a lender. But it's a good start. Armed with nothing more than this, I would begin trying to sell the house at market, which may be less than you owe.

If you are successful and do find a buyer ready, willing, and able to purchase on a short sale, write up the deal (or have your agent write it), get a deposit, and present it to the lender. From the lender's perspective, it's really tough to turn such a deal down, provided the amount short is not too great. After all, you're offering a way out that's neat and clean. If the lender refuses, there's the dirty way, involving foreclosure and the costs of fixing up a property that the lender could get in damaged condition.

**TIP**

Work from a position of power and leverage. Don't try to get the lender to commit formally to a short sale and for a specific amount of money until you actually get a buyer in hand. Then you've got something to deal with.

## 4. Try Converting to a Rental

Here's an idea that works, sometimes. Instead of selling or losing the home to foreclosure, why not try renting it out until times get better? After all, it's certain that at some time in the future, your property is going to be worth more than it is today. Why not hang on until times improve?

Most sellers have three good reasons for not wanting to rent out the property. First, they want to be done with it, one way or another. It's an emotional anchor to be continually worrying about the house, what's going to happen to it. Better, many sellers say, to have done with it even if that means foreclosure. (Bad answer. See item 6 below.)

Second, many sellers have never been landlords. They may feel they're jumping from the frying pan into the fire. What if the tenants don't pay? What if they move out? What if they mess up the place? Worst of all, what if they don't pay, don't move, and mess up the place?

Of course it could happen. But I've been renting properties of all kinds for more than 30 years and quite frankly, if you take pains to screen tenants carefully, it almost never happens. (Try reading up on renting. My 1994 book *The Landlord's Trouble-Shooter* is one good place to start.)

Third, in most markets you can't rent a home for enough money to pay for the PITI. (That's mortgage principal, interest, taxes, and insurance.) In other words, it will cost you money out of pocket each month to keep the place and rent it.

True, but it's probably worth it to protect your credit. (Again, see item 6 below.) And you may be able to significantly increase the amount of rent you receive by doing a "lease/option," as discussed in Chapter 11.

Renting your house out may not seem like a good option, particularly when you may have to rent for several years before you're able to sell. But it might be a terrific solution, compared with the alternatives. For more details on this option, check into Chapter 12.

## 5. Bite the Bullet and Change Your Plans

This is the least attractive alternative for most upside-down sellers. It means that you let your property dictate your future, instead of the other way round.

Some sellers, realizing that they can't sell or easily get out from under, have refused job transfers, have taken lower-paying jobs, have borrowed money (from the bank or relatives)—all so that they could stay were they were, in their home. They don't sell, and they do continue to make their payments.

This might mean using up some of the retirement money or the kids' college funds. It could mean a lesser lifestyle, for a while. It could mean remaining in an area after your friends have all moved away.

But it could also mean avoiding foreclosure and the trauma of a forced home move.

**TRAP**

Sometimes sellers just don't want to lose their "equity." They figure if they stay long enough, they'll get out what they have put into the house.

Bad move. It's usually possible to buy elsewhere, in a better market, and double or triple your equity in the time it takes to recoup it from an upside-down property.

**TIP**

Quite frankly, I don't recommend staying on, unless there's a compelling reason to preserve your ownership of the property. Personally, I prefer moving on with my life, even if it means using one of the more dramatic solutions noted above. I wouldn't like the trapped feeling of knowing that I couldn't move, yet was just afloat where I was. Better to take a hit now and get on with things.

## 6. Protect Your Mortgage Credit

Faced with difficult choices, a great many people who are upside down with their homes, choose to "walk." This is an unexpected application of the motto "When the going gets tough, the tough get going!" It's so much easier just to let the bank take the house back.

Yes it is—until you want to buy another house. Then you may find that you've thrown the baby out with the bath water. The truth is that the worst possible thing you could do, in terms of personal finance, is to allow a foreclosure to occur. The reason is that the foreclosure could preclude you from getting financing on another house anytime in the future.

"Isn't that a bit harsh?" you may be saying. After all, if a person goes through bankruptcy, within a few years of steady and on-time paying off bills, he or she can usually get a credit card and start establishing good credit for loans. In many cases the bankruptcy itself is taken "off the books" after 7 years.

Perhaps. But mortgage lenders are not credit card lenders. They have a different mentality and they have memories like elephants. To understand, for a moment look at it from their perspective.

Say you loan a friend $1000 that she agrees to repay with interest. Only she runs into hard times. She isn't able to make the payments for a while. But she struggles and struggles and eventually pays you back every dime, not including the interest.

Now, she wants to borrow again. Will you lend to her?

I would. This is a gal who will keep her bond. Even though things might not work out the way she plans, I'll feel confident I'll get my money back eventually.

On the other hand, you have another friend who also borrows $1000. When times get tough for him, he walks away from your loan. He never pays you back.

Now he's flush again and wants to borrow more money. He says everything is financially great with him and he'll have no trouble repaying. He'll even pay you extra interest. Will you lend to him?

Not me. I'll never feel secure again with this person. I'll always worry that if times get tough, he'll take the easy way out and forget about my loan.

Mortgage lenders are much the same way. They don't really care all that deeply if you have a bankruptcy or if you don't make payments on your credit cards. They'll look aside if you don't pay your telephone bill, or your water and electric bills. Just have a few good years of steady payments and they'll forgive all the bad times.

But if they ever find out you let a house go to foreclosure, most will never let you have another mortgage.

The reasoning here is that foreclosure is not like anything else. Lenders see it as a commitment on their part and yours. They will lend you more money than you could ever qualify for otherwise on your income. And, they anticipate, you will pay it back honorably, no matter what.

**TRAP**

The lender's doctrine: A borrower who learns to live with one foreclosure can live with many more.

All of which is to say that if you ever hope to buy another house in the future, protect your mortgage credit. Find a way to pay off the mortgage. Get yourself off the hook. Don't ever consider walking. If you do, you'll find it very difficult to get another mortgage in the future.

Of course, this is not to say that you can't ever get any kind of mortgage. Some conventional lender may get desperate and give you a loan. And there are always the "equity lenders" who will lend a small percentage of a property's value, and they don't care who's applying for the loan. Some don't even conduct a credit check. (They hope you won't make payments so they can foreclose!) But equity lenders require that you make a huge down payment and they charge much higher interest. They are a poor alternative.

### TIP

Don't think you can sneak by a lender. Every mortgage loan application asks if you have *ever* had a foreclosure. Most, today, also ask if you have ever given a deed in lieu of foreclosure (considered bad, but not nearly as bad as foreclosure). If you fudge on the application, the foreclosure could show up on a credit report. (Mortgage lenders use the most sophisticated nationwide credit reporting available.) Even if it doesn't show up and you do get the loan, should you later default and it turns out that you lied on your application, you could be liable for serious civil and/or criminal penalties.

### TRAP

Unless you obtained the mortgage as part of the purchase price and only in those states which have "purchase money mortgage" laws, even if you walk, the lender could go to court and obtain a deficiency judgment against you for any money it loses by taking the property. This judgment would follow you.

### Avoid the Mortgage Credit Trap

In almost all cases it is possible to avoid foreclosure. It may not be easy. You may need to change your plans or take actions you'd rather avoid. You may even have to sell an item you love, like a boat or car, to raise money for mortgage payments. You may have to do things you disdain, like borrowing from relatives. But where there's a will there's a way. And this is one case where finding the way will bring you a much happier future.

Being upside down is distinctly unpleasant. But don't ever give up hope. Almost always there are ways out. You just have to hunt to find them.

# 3

# Finding an Agent Who Will Sell Your Home

There's an old adage in the real estate business that goes "Those who list, last." The meaning is that the key to success *for an agent* is to get as many listings as possible. As some of those listings sell, the agent is provided with a continual stream of income. Thus many agents have become quite adept at gathering listings. However, what's good for the agent may not necessarily be good for you.

**TIP**

The words broker, associate, salesperson, and agent are all part of the same family. They all mean a person licensed by the state to sell real estate. A *broker* can operate an office and work independently. An *associate* or a *salesperson* (the two terms are synonymous) means that even though the person has a license, it is not a full license. An associate or a salesperson must work for a broker, under that broker's license. It doesn't mean associates aren't good at selling. It usually means that either they haven't had enough experience yet to get a broker's license (most states require several years) or they are more comfortable working for someone else than for themselves. *Agent* is the generic term for any licensed real estate person—broker, salesperson, or associate.

The last thing you want to do is to list your property with an agent who "gathers" listings. Chances are that once you sign the listing agreement, that's the last you'll see of your agent. If some other agent sells the house, great. But don't count on that lister of yours to push your property.

## What Kind of Agent Do I Want?

You want an active agent. The key is to list with someone who takes a strong, active interest in your property. I have a friend, Sarah, who is what I consider to be the best real estate agent a seller could ever find.

Sarah is a broker who owns and operates her own office. She has only about three (the number varies) salespeople working for her at any given time, so she doesn't have to be constantly supervising them. Instead, she handles property directly on her own. Sarah is what I call a "full service" agent. She lists property and she also sells it.

Sarah has been in business for about 15 years and she knows her community like the post office does. If you give her the address of your home (assuming it's in her community), frequently she can tell you off the top of her head what nearby houses have sold for in the last year or two. With just a walk through your home, she can give you a sales price that I would bank on. Sarah is that good.

Of course, the real reason that Sarah is so good at what she does is that she loves to sell real estate. For her it isn't work, it's pleasure. She's up by seven every morning, out in the field going to see the properties newly listed by other brokers and placed on the Multiple Listing Service. In the afternoons and evenings and on weekends, when buyers usually call off her ads, she quickly hooks their interest with her knowledge, qualifies them, and then takes them to see properties—of course, pushing her own listings first. She also pushes her listings to other brokers, talking the properties up at weekly broker meetings. She gives her listings the widest possible circulation in terms of letting brokers, as well as potential buyers, know they're for sale.

Sarah has an enviable track record. She has sold over 90 percent of all properties she has ever listed, even in bad markets! Nearly all those sales came within a few months of the listing date.

Would I list with her? You bet, in a moment, without a second's hesitation.

The question for you is: How do you find an agent like Sarah to list your home?

## How Do I Locate a Good Agent?

For many of us who don't know a "Sarah," the place we usually turn to is the yellow pages of the phone book. There are better ways, as we'll see later in this chapter. But for now, let's consider what you do see if you look in the yellow pages. Chances are that if you're new to real estate, you'll see names of independent offices which you may not recognize, as well as the names of franchise offices which may be very familiar to you. Some of the franchise advertising may be quite big. Many sellers simply "save time" and go with the known, the franchise name that they've heard before.

### Franchise or Independent?

Twenty years ago virtually all real estate agents were independent. Today, the majority belong to a franchise such as Century 21, R/EMAX, or Coldwell Banker. These are big names and big companies. Thus, one of the first questions that most sellers ask is: Should I go with a franchise or with an independent?

The answer is that the question is irrelevant. One of the best tips this book can give you is that you should go with the best agent you can find. If that agent happens to be associated with a franchise, great. If the agent is independent (as Sarah was), just as great. Don't base your listing decision solely on the sign in front of the office. Here's why.

In nearly all states, a real estate office must be operated by a broker licensed in that state. The licensed broker has the choice of hanging out a shingle with her or his name on it (or some other dba—made-up name) or buying into one of the many national franchises.

Many brokers opt for the franchise. The reason is quite simple. Let's take an example from the fast-food business. You drive into a town you've never been in before. You want something to eat. You want the meal to be fast and inexpensive, the premises to be clean and pleasant, and the food to be safe and at least minimally tasty. How are you going to pick?

You could take your chances with the local diner or you could stop at a few stores and ask people their opinions. Or you could drive directly to McDonald's, Burger King, Wendy's, or the like.

The national fast-food chains all maintain standards so that whether you go into one in Seattle or in Orlando, you know you'll get the same quality of service and food. (One of the most surprising fast-food visits I ever made was to a jam-packed Burger King on the Champs Elysées in Paris. The food was extraordinaire!)

A real estate franchisee affords the same name recognition and resulting business. Most real estate franchisers offer their franchisees advertising support, office management help, forms, even colorful jackets in addition to their signs and "colors." I know many real estate brokers who have doubled their income overnight by converting from being independent to being a franchise.

That's what a franchise offers brokers and why so many participate. The real question, of course, is what a franchise offers *you*.

## Pluses of a Franchise for You

As just discussed, franchises offer at least a minimal standard of performance. One office tends to look like another, and in general the agents tend to be fairly well trained. In addition, franchises offer long-distance moving assistance. List your home with a franchise in one city and an agent from a linked franchise in another city can already be looking for a new home for you.

In my opinion, the true value of the franchise is that it brings a degree of order, of homogeneity to real estate.

## Independent Pluses

On the other hand, there are the independents. They have limited advertising and name recognition. To make up for this they usually have to work harder.

**TIP**

Just because an office is independent many people conclude that the agents have to be better in order to make it on their own. This doesn't necessarily have to be true. The agents could just as easily be so terrible that no franchise would take them! On the other hand, a very good salesperson (or group of them) could be working for herself and simply not want to give a percentage of each deal to the franchise company.

What's important to understand, however, is that where it counts, in selling, the independents usually can offer just as much as the franchises. The reason is the listing services.

Usually both the independents and the franchise offices belong to the same listing services (typically the MLS—Multiple Listing Service) in their area, and since nearly all houses are listed on the services, all agents whether independent or franchised usually work on the same properties.

**TRAP**

That's not always the case. A recent trend has been for large franchise companies to hold some of their own listings (typically the better ones) just for their agents. Further, competing listing services have very recently begun popping up in large metropolitan areas. Thus, not every agent may be able to easily show you every listing. (However, if you want to see a particular house, your agent can call the lister, who will usually cooperate.)

## Answers to Questions on Franchises Versus Independents

I'm sure that you still have some questions regarding the choice between franchise and independent, so I've tried to anticipate them—and supply you with answers.

### Won't the Franchise Offer Better Service?

The franchise can offer name recognition, trained personnel, and usually more advertising. That doesn't necessarily translate into better service for you. Selling real estate remains a highly individualized operation. Remember, it's how much your lister pushes your property that counts. (We'll have more to say about this in Chapter 6.)

### Will the Franchise Back Up Its Salespeople's Actions?

Good question. Be sure to ask the franchisee. Some do, at least minimally. Some don't. It depends on what the problem is.

### What If an Independent Makes a Mistake That Costs Me Money?

Today nearly all real estate agents carry errors and omissions insurance as well as some form of malpractice insurance. In addition, California and some other states maintain funds to at least partially compensate people who have been victimized by bad agents. Ask your independent what protections are offered.

### My Choice

My own preference, as noted at the beginning of this section, is to pay little or no attention to the sign in front of the office. Instead, I judge the person I'm dealing with.

It's important to understand that this discussion is not intended to knock or praise either franchises or independents. I repeat, my advice is to go with the best agent you can find.

## How Do I Select a Good Agent?

A good first step is to ask your friends if they know people who have recently sold their home. There are so many agents around (close to 1 percent of the population in some areas) that almost everyone knows one. Did the sellers have a good experience? Ask them if they would recommend the agent. Ask them if they have any reservations about the agent.

## TRAP

Know your friends. Some agents pay a "finder's fee" to former clients who will recommend them to sellers. A good friend is more interested in your well-being than in a few bucks for a finder's fee. Just be sure you're dealing with a good friend.

### Interview Prospective Agents

If you can't get a recommendation, then it's up to you to find an agent. That's easy. Just put an FSBO (for sale by owner) sign on your front lawn. You'll have agents climbing all over you trying to get your listing. Finding a *good* agent, however, is a bit more difficult.

I don't recommend starting out with a sign on your front lawn. Rather, pick a real estate office that's nearby and check it out. Walk in and tell the receptionist or the salesperson who greets you that you want to talk to the broker. (Don't explain why, yet.)

When the broker appears, explain that you are *thinking* of listing your house. You want to list with an office that's *active*. In fact, you'd like to list with the best salesperson (not lister) in the office. But for now, you want to learn something about the office itself.

For example, how many listings does the office currently have? If the office is active, the broker will be delighted to point out the many listings. If the office is a dud, there won't be many or any. Leave.

## TRAP

Be sure to ask for listings taken by agents in this office. Don't be fooled if the broker simply takes out a book and shows you all the listings on the MLS. None of them may belong to that office.

Now ask how many of its *own listings this office* has sold in the past 6 months. The broker should know exactly. If the agents haven't sold any, or there's any hemming and hawing, leave.

Along the way, listen carefully to what the broker says. Is there one name, one agent, who keeps popping up? Is that agent, in fact, the best seller in the office?

At the end of your brief discussion, ask the broker who would be the best seller in the office in terms of sales (not listings) made. Most brokers will chuckle at your audacity, but will also probably give you a straight answer. (Is it the same name that kept popping up in your earlier conversation?)

Now go see that person. Introduce yourself and ask not only how many properties he or she has sold, but how many were listed in the past 6 months. (You want to deal with a good salesperson, but also one who handles listings, not just the sales end of the business.)

Ask if you can have a list with phone numbers of the sellers of listings that this agent recently sold. Explain that you'd like to call them to see what they thought of the service.

This is the acid test. Most sellers never ask to see such a list. They wouldn't think of it. After all, it sounds like you're asking to see something confidential.

**TIP**

It's not confidential. Sales of homes are all recorded and are all public knowledge. If you want to take the time to go down to the courthouse, you can compile your own list of recent sellers.

A strong agent, one who will work for you, will be *delighted* to give you a list of recent sellers. After all, what does the agent do but please clients? A weak agent will give you reasons that she or he can't give out the list. Leave.

**TIP**

In some offices, particularly the larger ones, the names of top agents, and in some cases even their pictures, often are posted on the walls. Just look carefully as you enter, and your questions may be answered.

### Find Out About the Agent

While knowing that the agent is a great salesperson is an enormous plus for you, you also need to know something more about him or her. You want to be sure the person is competent in the real estate business, is honest in dealings, and is reliable.

You may want to ask the following questions to help you determine these things.

1. *"How long have you been in the real estate business?"* The learning curve for real estate is fairly long. The reason is that the number of transactions a person can become involved with at any one time is limited. Usually it takes 3 to 5 years for an agent to have gotten a well-rounded education; 5 to 10 years is better.

2. *"What professional organizations do you belong to?"* The minimum here should be the local real estate board and multiple listing service, as well as the state and National Association of Realtors® (NAR). The agent may also be a member of the chamber of commerce and local citizens' committees—all pluses.

3. *"What will you do to expedite the sale of my home?"* The answer here should be immediate, direct, and comprehensive. The agent should explain a plan of action that he or she hopes will sell your house. The plan should include:
   A. Listing for a specified time. (Beware of agents who want to list for more than 3 months except in a cool or cold market.)
   B. Promotion, including talking up the listing at the local real estate board.
   C. Advertising.
   D. Open houses.

These, then, are some of the questions you can ask of your future agent. Here's a checklist to take with you when you interview an agent.

### Checklist for Interviewing Agents

1. Houses listed in the last 6 months. _____

2. Houses sold in the last 6 months. _____

|  | YES | NO |
| --- | --- | --- |
| 3. References available? | [ ] | [ ] |

|                                                                      | YES | NO  |
|----------------------------------------------------------------------|-----|-----|
| 4. Agent fully licensed?                                             | [ ] | [ ] |
| 5. Has been in the real estate business at least 3 to 5 years?       | [ ] | [ ] |
| 6. Belongs to many professional organizations?                       | [ ] | [ ] |
| 7. Offers a plan for selling my home?                                | [ ] | [ ] |
| 8. Does not ask for an overly long listing?                          | [ ] | [ ] |

## If I Agree to List, What Does the Agent Owe Me in Return?

Listing your home for sale is not a one-way street. You agree to pay a hefty commission to the agent. But that agent also agrees to give you something in return. That something includes:

Service

Loyalty

Diligence

Honesty

Disclosure of facts

Skill

Care

Some of the above may actually be stated in the listing agreement. Others are considered part of the agent's fiduciary responsibilities. All are considered examples of ethical conduct.

### Different Agents, Different Duties

When you list with an agent, he or she owes you loyalty. That takes many forms. The clearest expression of loyalty is when that same agent gets a sales agreement of, say, $90,000 from buyers, but tells you that she or he has overheard the buyers say they would be willing to pay $95,000 for the house.

That little bit of information is worth $5000. Without it, you might have accepted the $90,000 offer. With it you hold out for $95,000—and get it.

Why should the agent be loyal to you and not to the buyer? Why should the agent tell you this little tidbit of information that was worth so much money?

The reason has to do with the agent's fiduciary (position of trust) relationship with you. It is incumbent upon the agent to tell you any fact that may help you in making your decision to sell.

On the other hand, if you tell the agent that you would be willing to accept $85,000 when you're asking $90,000, the agent is not obliged to tell that fact to the buyers. In fact, because of the fiduciary relationship, the agent is prohibited (in theory) from telling the buyers anything about price or terms that you do not specifically tell the agent to divulge.

In other words, the agent is bound to you in ways that are definitely to your advantage. However, it's important not to get too smug about agency relationships. Not all agents stick to the letter of ethical conduct, and some agents (buyers' agents) may have fiduciary responsibilities to the buyers and not to you.

## What Are Subagents?

When you list your property with an agent, he or she owes you a fiduciary responsibility as described above. But what if the agent puts your property on the listing service and suddenly 100 or 1000 agents are all working it? Do they owe you a fiduciary responsibility?

Yes—and no.

If they act as "subagents" (meaning that your agent delegates agency powers to them), then they owe you the same duties and responsibilities. They owe it to you to tell you when the buyers are willing to pay more, and not to tell the buyers when you are willing to take less.

However, some agents act independently, although they may still show your house and sell it off the listing service. These agents may work either for you and for the buyers or just for the buyers alone.

## Dual Agents

A dual agent is one who not only works for you the seller, but also works for the buyer. The dual agent represents both parties. The crux of a dual agent's responsibilities can be found (just like the seller's agent's could) in the price. A dual agent may not tell a buyer that you're willing to take less *or tell you that the buyer is willing to pay more.*

In other words, the dual agent, because he or she owes both you and the buyer loyalty, forgoes disclosing price information to either of you (and other information, such as who's willing to concede terms). A dual agent must disclose his or her status to you.

### Buyer's Agents

Finally, there is the matter of an agent who works exclusively for the buyer. What's confusing is that a buyer's agent may also work off the listing sheet that your selling agent put your home on. However, this agent owes a fiduciary responsibility to the buyer. In the case of price, the buyer's agent is required to tell the buyer if he or she learns you are willing to take less, but is not required to tell you if the buyer is willing to pay more.

Thus there are in reality three separate levels of agent with corresponding duties:

| | |
|---|---|
| Seller's (listing) agent | Fiduciary to seller |
| Dual agent | Fiduciary to buyer and seller |
| Buyer's agent | Fiduciary to buyer |

The real question is: How do you know with whom you're dealing? If you're dealing with your seller's agent, you can feel comfortable confiding everything (presuming the agent is honest and follows his or her fiduciary duties). On the other hand if you're dealing with the buyer's agent, you should not confide anything, because every stray word that passes your lips will find its way back to the buyer. How do you know whom to trust?

**TIP**

Many sellers mistakenly believe that the payment of a commission determines the type of agent. For example, you pay the broker; therefore, automatically the broker is a seller's agent. Not so. Many real estate regulating agencies have held that who pays the commission is irrelevant.

## Get an Agent's Disclosure Statement

In the old days (several decades ago) the National Association of Realtors® offered a code of ethics that was the forerunner of many of the rules of agency in most states. The code of ethics basically required that the agent deal fairly with all parties, both buyers and sellers.

Today, however, an increasing number of states are requiring that agents disclose to you whom they represent.

Thus, when you sign your listing agreement, the agent may also present to you a second document which states, in effect, one of the following:

> I am a seller's agent with the following duties and responsibilities to you....and I have a duty to disclose to you all facts affecting the value of the property.

> OR

> I am a dual agent and I represent both buyers and sellers. I may not disclose to you if a buyer is willing to pay more than the offered price.

> OR

> I am a buyer's agent and I represent the buyer and I owe that buyer a fiduciary responsibility and I may not disclose to you if a buyer is willing to pay more than the offered price.

Usually you must not only read the disclosure, but sign that you understand what it says. (There's nothing wrong with signing— just be sure that you do, in fact, understand what the disclosure says.)

## Which Type of Agent Do I Want?

The question which arises out of all of this is: Which kind of agent do you want? The answer is simple. When you're selling your house you want only a seller's agent. You want to be sure that the person with whom you list will represent you thoroughly.

That's all well and good. But what happens when your agent goes out and brings in a buyer (no other agent involved)? Does your agent now become a *dual* agent?

Maybe. It all comes out in disclosure. The agent who brings you the offer on your house should disclose what type of agent she or he is. If they don't disclose, you should demand a disclosure.

**TIP**

Whenever an offer is presented, demand to know who the agent presenting the offer represents. The agent should tell you. If the agent doesn't, presume that person is acting for the buyer and treat the offer adversarially. Keep a tight lip and don't blab what you might take, if it's less than is being offered.

The point to understand here is that the agent determines whom she or he represents. Your goal is to find out who it is and then act accordingly.

# 4

# What Is a Realistic Price for Your Home?

What is your home worth?

As noted in the first chapter, price for real estate is mainly determined by the marketplace. If one of two identical homes, both in the same location, sells for $125,000, then presumably the other is also worth $125,000.

The trouble is that seldom are two homes identical, and even if they are both in the same neighborhood, almost never are their locations exactly equal. (One may be on a busier street, the other closer to a park, and so on.)

Thus determining price becomes as much judgment as science. In this chapter we're going to see how to compare your property with recent home sales to get the most realistic price possible.

### TRAP

Remember, the cardinal rule is that a realistic price has nothing to do with what you owe, what you've put into the property, or what you "feel" it should be worth. Price is only what the market will bear.

## How Do I Find Out What Comparable Homes Have Recently Sold For?

This is known as having market knowledge. Surprisingly, it's quite easy to obtain, even though when you start you may be completely blind to what the true market for homes in your area is like. After all, just because you live in Nashville, for example, is no reason for you to have any detailed knowledge of the Nashville housing market. Yes, you may have heard about some neighbors down the street who sold for a certain price, but was their home just like yours? What about other homes that have sold more recently for more money—or less? What you need is to get a good handle on competitive housing prices in your area.

### TIP

 Become a pretend buyer for a weekend to quickly gain a better knowledge of the housing market in your area. Go around with a broker (or by yourself to open houses) and see what's out there. It won't take you very long at all to begin sizing up the market.

### Don't Try to Reinvent the Wheel

The one most important thing that every real estate agent learns is the market. No agent worth his or her salt is ignorant of prices. Therefore, why not tap into that readily available knowledge? I'm not suggesting you call a broker to list your house. (See Chapter 3 for information on doing that.) Just that you contact an agent for information.

Remember, agents are anxious to please you. They hope that by helping you in every way that they can, when you finally do decide to list, you'll give them the listing. Take advantage of their generosity. (And you may discover an agent with whom you'd like to list!)

Here's what to ask the agent: "I'm thinking of putting my house up for sale. I want to ask a competitive price. Can you supply me with a list of *comparables* for my home?"

What you are asking for is a list of homes that have recently sold and the sales prices (and original listing prices) of homes that are similar to yours. If you just compare the houses on this list with your home, you'll almost instantly have a pretty good idea of the market.

Providing you with such a list is the easiest of things for an agent to do. Virtually all areas of the country have listing services (such as the Multiple Listing Service), and nearly all agents belong to them. Today these listing service groups are computerized, and their databanks can provide members with all kinds of lists, including those for sales and houses currently for sale going back months, sometimes years.

These lists can be chosen by neighborhood, by price, by type of house, and so on. On most services, the agent, with the tap of a few buttons on a computer, can print out a list of comparable homes sold in your section of town, your neighborhood, even your street.

## How Do I Read a List of Comparables?

Once you have a list of comparables, you must do two things. First, you must analyze the list itself. That means you must make a judgment call about which homes that have been recently sold are actually similar to yours and which are not. Then I suggest you drive by several of the most apparently comparable homes to confirm your choices. Let's analyze the list first.

### Doing a Gross Analysis

When you get the list of comparables, first check that they have the same number of bedrooms, baths, pool (if you have one), and other amenities as your home. Eliminate those houses that are obviously dissimilar.

Next, if there is one sale on the list that seems suspiciously low compared with the others and another suspiciously high, throw them out. Chances are there was something unusual about the sale that you may never know about. (The seller was divorcing and had to take the first offer no matter how low, or the buyer fell in love with the property and paid far too much for it.)

### TRAP

Most sellers looking at a list of comparables automatically let their eyes fall on the highest-priced home there and then figure that's what their own home is worth. It's only natural to think your property is worth top dollar. But will buyers really see it that way?

### Look for *Recent* Sales

The real estate market is constantly in a state of flux. Prices that are more than 6 months old may be out of date. Your house could be worth considerably more—or less.

Also, beware of looking at list prices. (Many times the inventory of homes you receive will include both sales and listings.) The list price of houses currently on the market can be deceptive. Most of the homes currently for sale will *not* sell for their listed price. Eventually the sellers will get desperate and reduce their price or, if they insist on an unrealistic value, they may simply take their home off the market.

List price is what the seller is "asking." Rarely, except in very hot markets, does the seller get that amount. To look only at asking prices of houses currently listed can give you a false sense of value.

### How Much Lower Than List Are Homes Selling For?

Try to do a comparison of at least six homes. Write down both their listed and their sales prices. Now take your calculator and do a little math. Divide the *sales price into the listing price* for those half dozen homes. This will give you the percentage difference between the asking (list) price and the sales price.

**TIP**

Knowing the percentage difference between list and sales prices tells you how active the market is as well as how much less than your asking price you can expect to sell your home for. (It will tell you, in effect, the market's condition.)

Analyzing the Percentage Differential

| Listing Price | Sales Price | % Difference |
|---|---|---|
| $114,000 | $109,000 | −4 |
| 120,000 | 108,000 | −10 |
| 115,000 | 106,000 | −8 |
| 118,000 | 110,000 | −7 |
| 112,000 | 109,000 | −3 |
| 105,000 | 107,000 | +2 |
| Average $114,000 | $108,000 | 5.5 |

Note that although the listing prices range from $105,000 to 120,000—a $15,000 range—the sales prices range only from $106,000 to $110,000—a $4000 range. In other words, though sellers can ask what they want, buyers have determined that the homes are only worth around $108,000. Also note that in one case, a home priced too low sold for more, probably because of multiple offers. Finally, notice that the average difference between listing and sales price was about 5 percent—a common figure in most areas of the country in a stable market.

## What Does the Percentage Difference Tell You?

The percentage difference between list and sales prices tells you a number of things, including how realistic the asking prices for homes are in the area, how strong or weak the market is, and, indirectly, how long it may take to sell your home.

- If the average percentage difference is less than 5 percent, you're in a healthy market. If your price is realistic, you'll get close to it and it shouldn't take long to sell.

- If the percentage differences are between 5 and 10 percent, you're in a soft market. Sellers aren't getting what they feel their homes are worth. Homes probably aren't selling quickly. To get a quick sale, you'll probably need to drop your price.

- If the percentage differences are between 10 and 20 percent, the market is very weak. Few homes are selling—only those at fire-sale prices, probably picked up by speculators. You probably won't be able to sell your home at what you consider its true value in this market.

## Confirm the Time Lag

The percentage difference between list and sales prices will also suggest the time lag, or how long it takes between listing and selling your home. Typically the higher the percentage, the longer the time lag.

You can confirm this by asking your agent for a list detailing the date the properties were listed and the date they were sold. You can quickly calculate the time it took between listing and sales for the homes you've checked as comparables. (Some listing services have already prepared an average time figure—the average time a listed house is on the market before a sale. For example, the service may say the current average is 2 months between listing and sale, or 6 months or a year.)

### TRAP

The agent may not be able to provide you with a list of how long houses currently listed, though not yet sold, have been on the market. The reason is that a buyer could use this list to pick out houses that had been up for sale for the longest time and concentrate on making lowball offers to those owners. An agent helping a buyer do this might be in a conflict of interest with a seller.

Any time lag under 2 months for an average sale is considered a very good market. Over 3 months is a soft market. Over 6 months is a very weak market.

## Should I Check Out the Houses on My Comp List?

Absolutely yes!

You've got a list of six (or however many) sales of homes that you believe are comparable to yours. But are they really? Maybe they're all painted purple, have terrible landscaping, or are on awkward-shaped lots on heavily trafficked streets. Maybe they aren't at all like your home; maybe their condition and location within the neighborhood makes them much worse—or better!

Check them out.

It won't take that long to drive by, and with just a glance you can upgrade or downgrade them in terms of how comparable they truly are. Don't skip this important step.

## What Price Should I Set for My House?

Should you ask the average sales price, the average list price, or an in-between figure when you put your house up for sale?

My suggestion is that, when possible and depending on your own needs, ask at least the average *list price.* If you ask the average listing price, you can expect to get the average sales price.

Remember, however, that in reality, average list and sales prices are only indicators, clues, hints. Your house may be much better (or worse) than the average, and you can ask and get more (or less) depending on condition.

### TRAP

Don't make the mistake of listing your home for the average sales price. Except in a hot market, buyers don't offer list price; they tend to offer less. If you ask the average sales price, you'll tend to get even lower offers and you could end up selling for less than you hoped for. To get the average sales price, you normally have to ask the average list price.

## Making the Price Decision

Finally, it's time to decide on a realistic price (one that will attract a buyer within a reasonable amount of time). You'll need to consider the market and comparables. Then you'll have to add or subtract according to the value of your particular home. Use the following guide to help you make your pricing decision.

### Pricing Decision Guide

Average sales price of comparables - - - - - - - - - - - - - - - -> $_____

|                              | Add     | Subtract |
|------------------------------|---------|----------|
| 1. Better/worse neighborhood | $_____ | $_____  |
| 2. Older/younger home        | $_____ | $_____  |

| | | |
|---|---|---|
| 3. Better/worse condition | $_____ | $_____ |
| 4. Other factors pro/con | $_____ | $_____ |
| Totals | $_____ | $_____ |

Add/subtract for comparables - - - - - - - - - - - - - - - - ->+/-$_____

The true market price - - - - - - - - - - - - - - - - - - - - - - - - - -> $_____

## Is the Price Too Low?

I can remember once going into a home that was owned by an elderly gentleman who had emphysema. He made it quite plain that the only real investment he had in the world was his house and that he wanted to sell it to me. He carefully explained that he had the following mortgages on the house:

| | |
|---|---|
| First | $55,000 |
| Second | 15,000 |
| Third | 5,000 |
| Fourth | 6,000 |
| | $81,000 |

He explained that he had so much indebtedness on the property because of his illness. He had borrowed to pay hospital bills. The third and fourth mortgages were actually liens put on his property by a doctor and a nursing home.

He then went on to explain that he needed to get $50,000 cash out of his house. He needed that to pay for his continuing medical treatment. If I could find someone to give him that money, he would sign in a minute.

I had already checked comparables, the neighborhood, and the condition of his house. In my opinion, it wasn't worth more than $85,000, tops. He really didn't even have enough equity to pay his normal closing costs, let alone realize $50,000 cash from the sale. I didn't see how he could get any cash at all out.

As carefully as I could, I tried to explain the *realities* of the situation to him. He listened patiently until I was finished and then said, "That's all well and good. But I still need to get $50,000 out of the sale!"

The point here is that what you can afford (or want) to sell your home for, unfortunately, is irrelevant when it comes time to sell.

The sales price is determined by what a buyer who is ready, willing, and able will pay for the property. The fact that you have it mortgaged for than that amount or that you want specific cash out for more than the realistic sales prices just doesn't matter.

It's a shame, it's sometimes sad, but it's the facts as they are. As Jesse Livermore (who made $22 million in stocks during the Depression, then lost $20 million of it in commodities) once said, "There ain't no money lying on the streets and if there was, ain't nobody shoveling it into your pocket." The market ultimately determines the highest sales price you will be able to get for your house.

## Is the Market Price Something You Can Live With?

At the beginning of this chapter you were asked to become a pretend buyer for a weekend and look at the market. For readers who did that, I'm sure it was an education in itself. After visiting an agent and getting sales and list prices, you should have an even better idea of the market. Finally, after going through the above guide you should have a dollar amount that expresses what you can realistically get for your home.

Is it a figure you can live with? Or is it so far out of bounds in terms of what you want and need that you're ready to throw your hands up in frustration?

If you can't live with the realistic price, I suggest you reread Chapter 2. It gives suggestions about alternatives to selling, including renting out your home for a time or continuing to live in it.

### TRAP

Don't get sidetracked when friends or agents suggest using other approaches to evaluating your house. There are a variety of other methods (besides looking at comparables) for analyzing the value of property. For example, the "cost approach" determines value by the cost of rebuilding. The "income approach" determines value by the potential rental income of the house.

Forget such methods. They are great for income-producing investment property. But for residential real estate, there is only one realistic approach and that is to check comparables as shown here. The comparable method is not only the approach preferred by competent appraisers, it is the one that lenders almost entirely rely upon.

## Should I Consult an Appraiser?

You've done your homework and you have an excellent idea of what your house is worth. But you're still not sure. You would like the stamp of approval of a professional. It's time to call in an appraiser.

You can get an appraiser to give you a qualified *opinion* as to the value of your house. The cost is usually under $500, often much less. Look for an appraiser in the phone book under that heading. Find an appraiser who has either an AMI or SREA designation.

A registered appraiser should give you a lengthy written opinion of value. It will undoubtedly take into account comparables as well as, perhaps, the cost and the income approaches. Of course, the bottom line is that the appraisal will give you, presumably, one figure—the value of your home. See how it compares with the figure you arrived at by checking comparables on your own.

You can also get a broker to give you an opinion as to the value of your home. Most brokers will do this for free in the hopes of getting a listing out of you. (Of course you need not list just to get an appraisal.)

### TRAP

If you want to have a broker appraise your property, make sure that he or she gives you a *written* appraisal and that it is understood up front that there will be no charge. Some agents will offer appraisals, then send the owner a bill for several hundred dollars for the "work." These agents are not in the business of selling real estate, but in the business of making appraisals.

Beware of them. Be sure you have it in writing that either the appraisal is free or that, if there is a charge, you know up front what it is and that you agree to it. (Quite frankly, I would not normally pay for any appraisal given by a real estate agent or anyone else who was not a professional appraiser.)

Most brokers who are willing to give you an appraisal just use the comparable approach described above. Typically even before they come out to meet you they've looked up your neighborhood and comparables for your size home. Once at your house, they just check its condition and mentally knock off a few dollars or add a few on.

## Why Not Just Use the Broker's Appraisal?

You may be asking yourself, "If an agent can give me an appraisal in just a few minutes, why bother going to all the trouble of doing it myself?"

The answer is confidence. Your own appraisal has one big advantage. You can totally trust yourself. You know the work you did and the effort you put forth.

Yes, it's nice to see if an appraiser and an agent roughly agree with you. (If they don't, you may want to check to see that you—or they—didn't make some gross error.) But if you do it yourself, you know how the price was arrived at. You're not worried that someone is trying to pull the wool over your eyes. That's really nice.

And just remember, later on when an agent or buyer tries to knock the price down, you'll have the confidence to hold to your guns because you'll *know* what your house is really worth.

# 5

# Negotiating a Better (for You) Commission

Everything in real estate is negotiable, including the commission. Once you've decided to list your home for sale and have found the right agent, it's time to negotiate the commission and the listing itself.

If this surprises you, you're not alone. Most first-time buyers and even a great many experienced ones aren't aware that commissions and listings are fully negotiable. They just assume there's a going rate and the agent will give them that.

Nothing could be further from the truth. There is no "going rate" and every agent will negotiate for the listing terms, conditions, and commission rate. Not every agent will necessarily accept what you may want to offer, but all agents should listen and consider it.

### TIP

If you find an agent who doesn't want to negotiate, listen carefully. Maybe, just maybe, the agent is so good that he or she can command a higher price. But before you list with any agents, you'd better have some pretty solid indications that they can deliver a buyer at your price and terms in short order.

### TRAP

It is both illegal and unethical in all areas of the country for a real estate board to "set" a minimum rate of commission. While this was done in some areas 30 or 40 years

ago, it's not done today. Lawsuits and judicial decisions
have outlawed that practice. If an agent tells you that you
must pay a "going rate" or a "set fee," find another agent.


## Can I Knock Down an Agent's Commission?

Most rates of commission today for single-family residential property range from a low of 3 percent to a high of 7 percent. Let's say
your agent walks in and says that she wants 7 percent. Should you
pay it?

I had this happen to me several years ago when I was selling a
house out of my area. The agent pointed out that, yes, the commission was negotiable. However, she was an excellent salesperson
and her track record with sales of listings proved it. True, other
offices in the area were asking only between 5 and 6 percent, but
she was better than they were. Was I willing, she asked, to pay a
lower rate and wait longer, perhaps forever, to sell my property?
Wouldn't it be cheaper to pay a higher rate and get a quicker, sure
sale?

I mention this example because the same type of argument may
be used on you. Be aware, however, that it's most often the lister
(agent who only lists) who uses it.

I asked the agent if she would guarantee me a sale. She said she
couldn't do that, but then again no one could. (*Note:* Some offices
will guarantee to buy your home at a predetermined price if you
don't sell within a set period of time. There could be inherent con-
flicts of interest here, as discussed later in this chapter.)

I asked if she could guarantee to sell my property faster than any
other agent. She said she was sure she could sell it quickly. She
couldn't guarantee that, but then again, nothing in this world had
a guarantee attached to it.

I then asked her why, if she couldn't guarantee anything, she felt
she was entitled to a commission higher than other reputable,
good agents were charging. She explained that it was because she
was better than they, in her opinion, and would work harder for
me.

I pointed out that each potential listing agent I talked with
stressed that she or he was better than others, that all said they

would work hard for a quick sale, and that, as far as I could tell, she wasn't offering anything more for the additional rate. Then I showed her to the door.

The point here is that while there's nothing wrong with paying a higher price for better service, if it is better service, it's a shame to pay that higher price for standard service.

## Negotiate Lower

There's no reason that you can't tell an agent what the maximum commission is that you'll pay. For example, you can say, "I'm willing to pay a 5 percent commission (or 4 percent or whatever). Are you willing to work for that amount?"

Now listen carefully to what the agent replies. Some will say that they can't afford to do a good job for that price and may decline and leave. That's probably an agent who knows what he or she is worth.

Others may say that, yes, they'll consider working for what you offer. But they can't perform all the normal tasks that go with selling. For a lower commission, they want you to do some of the work, such as showing the property or paying for some of the advertising. Again, this is probably an agent who knows what it costs to sell a home and is offering you a way to share those costs.

Finally, others may say that, yes, they'll accept that commission rate and work just as hard as they would for a higher rate. I would be suspicious of these types of agents. They may also know what they're worth—and it could be a lot less than the other agents in terms of ability to deliver a buyer ready, willing, and able to buy.

### TRAP

Beware of agents who accept an unusually low commission. They may intend to simply list your house on a Multiple Listing Service and let it go at that with no additional support. This is not an agent you want at any price.

Good agents will do one of three things. They will explain why they charge a certain rate and point out that they really can't afford to work for less. If you insist on less, they may accept the listing provided you understand they will in turn provide less than normal service. If you insist on paying less and insist on getting full service, they will refuse the listing.

### TIP

A good agent won't try to browbeat you into paying a higher commission. Good agents don't get rich by charging higher commissions or by making enemies of sellers. They get rich by making more deals.

While you don't want to try to "cheat" your agent into a low fee that will make him or her not want to serve you, you also don't want to pay an excessive fee either. My suggestion is that you check with several agents to see what most in your area are charging and pay no more—or less—than that.

### TRAP

Just because the commission is negotiable is not necessarily a good reason to insist on a low commission rate. You generally get what you pay for. If you offer a commission lower than your next-door neighbor who has the same house at roughly the same price, which house do you think agents will be more likely to show?

## Why Are Real Estate Commissions So High?

Even though the agent may make a good case for a commission, one can't help but wonder why commissions in general are so high. For example, back in the 1950s the commissions were generally around 5 percent. By the 1990s, as several studies have shown, the average commissions climbed to the 6 and sometimes 7 percent range.

In addition, back in the 1950s the average house cost only around $15,000. Today it's over $120,000. That means that back in

1950 an agent who sold a house for $15,000 at a 5 percent commission collected a total of only $750. Today an agent who sells a $120,000 house for 6 percent collects a commission of $7200. Today's commission is almost 10 times higher. Why?

There are three answers to this question.

1. Part of the answer is simple inflation. Things cost many times more today than they did 40 years ago.

2. Another part of the answer is better agents. Back in 1950 all an agent had to do to sell real estate was pass a short test, rent an office, and put out a sign. Today agents' tests often last several days. There may be college or night school requirements, and there may also be apprenticeship requirements. Even the cost of the license itself has gone up.

3. Finally, there are additional selling costs today. In the 1990s, agents must pay for errors and omission insurance as well as several kinds of malpractice insurance. Also, they must have an attorney on call, something that almost no one did back in 1950.

Thus if agents ask for a higher commission today than 40 years ago, there is some justification for it. Besides, the agent may not get the whole commission.

While you may deal with only one listing agent, by the time your house is sold, there may be as many as four agents involved. (In the vast majority of cases at least two agents are involved.)

Typically the commissions are split between agents. The splits vary with 50-50 being typical, although 60-40 splits (60 percent going to the selling agency and 40 percent to the listing) are also common.

Let's say you sell your home for $100,000. There happen to be two different brokers involved and two different salespeople. (You listed with a salesperson, the buyer bought through a salesperson.) Here's how a typical split of a 6 percent commission might work out:

| | | |
|---|---|---|
| 1.5% | $1500 | Listing salesperson |
| 1.5 | 1500 | Listing broker |
| 1.5 | 1500 | Selling salesperson |
| 1.5 | 1500 | Selling broker |
| 6% | $6000 | Total commission |

Instead of a whopping $6000 paid to one person, four agents each get $1500. If the agent is to make $30,000 a year selling houses, that means that he or she has to make 20 deals just like yours. That's a lot of deals for an agent.

It's important to understand that I'm not trying to justify higher commissions. It's simply a matter of pointing out that in many cases the commissions aren't as high as they would appear to be on the surface.

## Should I Use a Discount Broker?

In many areas of the country discount brokers are available. These brokers often charge a rate that may be half the normal commission rate. If the typical rate is, for example, 6 percent in your area, they may charge only 3 percent. On a $100,000 house that could mean the difference between a $6000 commission and a $3000 commission. It could save you $3000. Why not go with a discounter?

You can, and I suggest you do, if you're trying to sell your home by yourself as described in Chapter 8. A discounter may provide just the limited services that you need. But remember, it works best in a hot market. As the market cools off, the discounted listing becomes less and less appealing. The reason is that discounters also provide fewer services.

Consider this true experience. I was looking for a rental home to buy in a market that I could only describe as warm. I was working with an agent and he was showing me this house and that. I happened to glance over at his listing book (a book which contains pictures as well as listings of homes for sale) and noticed that he always seemed to skip over one page that contained homes presumably in the price range I was looking for.

After a time I asked him if I could look at that book. He hesitated, then complied. He explained he wasn't supposed to show it to someone who wasn't an agent in his area. I suspected he showed it to anyone who asked.

I immediately turned to that page he had been skipping. In addition to others, it contained two homes that looked ideal for my needs. I asked him why we hadn't looked at them. We could, he explained, only he didn't think they were right for me. When I looked closer at the listing, I saw that they were both listed by discounters for a 3 percent commission. The truth is, they weren't right for *him*!

## TIP

There are several kinds of agents, as we saw in the last chapter, but the agent showing buyers property owes a loyalty to them to show all the houses suitable for them. In theory, the agent should never shy away from a house which might be ideal for the buyers but which provides a lower commission. That's unethical and may even be illegal. The actual practice, however, is sometimes considerably different from the theory.

### Can You Handle the Reduced Service?

In addition to reducing the potential exposure to your property, many discount brokers reduce the services they offer to you. For example, they may not be willing to negotiate with the buyers for you. That could be up to you. Or they could ask you to pay for advertising (which, it may turn out, only benefits them). Or they may not be willing to work with buyers to secure financing or to move a deal through escrow.

In short, a discounter cannot afford to give you what a full-service broker offers, because you aren't paying enough. On the other hand, perhaps you don't need full service. Perhaps what you need is partial service, because you're selling your home on your own.

My advice is to let yourself be guided by your needs. If you want a broker to handle your sale, go to a full-service, full-commission broker. On the other hand, if you're an FSBO (for sale by owner) seller, then by all means try a discounter.

Here are some reasons that discounters may be good for you:

- You pay a lower commission.
- You don't need a full-service broker.

Here are the reasons that discounters may not be your best bet, even though you save money:

- Your house may get far lower exposure.
- There may be less advertising.
- You may have to pay for advertising.
- The agent may not handle critical paperwork or may not help the buyers secure financing.
- The agent may not help you in your negotiations with buyers, resulting ultimately in your receiving a lower price.

## What Is a Listing Agreement?

In addition to agreeing on a commission rate, there's the matter of agreeing to the terms of the listing. These are spelled out in a listing agreement that the agent will want you to sign.

There are a variety of listing types which an agent can offer you. (No, there isn't just one standard listing that they all use.) Each type of listing has its own pluses and minuses and should be considered in light of your specific needs. The listing agreement will normally say right on the face the type that it is. You can negotiate the type of listing agreement with the agent.

### Exclusive Right to Sell

An exclusive right-to-sell listing is the type that almost all agents prefer. It is also the type that many listing services prefer. It means the following:

*If the agent or anyone else (including you) sells the house, you owe the agent a commission.* This includes people to whom you showed the house while the listing was in effect, even though you sell the house for a period of time after the listing expires.

In other words, with this type of listing you ensure the agent a commission if the house is sold. The only way the agent cannot get a commission is if there is no sale. Sellers tend to dislike this type of commission because they feel it's unfair. Agents, on the other hand, like it because they feel protected. Most are willing to put forth 100 percent effort only if they get this type of listing.

### Exclusive Agency

*If the agent sells the house, you owe a commission. If you sell it to someone the agent didn't show it to, you don't owe anything.*

Now, you may be thinking, there's a listing that's more to my liking. Yes and no. Agents have good reasons for not liking this type of listing. They may bring buyers to your home who tell them they're not interested in purchasing. Later, the buyers come to you and negotiate a sale. You claim no commission is due because you had no knowledge that the agent showed these buyers the home; they dealt directly with you. The agent claims that a commission is due because he or she found the buyer.

In this case, the agent is right. But to get that commission the agent might have to go to arbitration or even to court. Along the way there's certain to be hard feelings, and agents are very concerned about their reputation in a community. They don't like it to be known that they're having to put pressure on to collect even a justified commission. Thus most agents simply won't work (or won't work hard) on this type of listing.

An exclusive agency listing is sometimes appropriately used when you have a buyer or buyers who you think might be interested in purchasing, but who haven't yet committed. You want to list the property and get it onto the market, but you want to exclude paying a commission for those buyers you've already found.

### Open Listing

*You agree to pay a commission to any broker who brings you a buyer or to pay no commission if you find the buyer.* Some sellers think this is a good type of listing, because you can give it to any agent.

Most agents, however, won't devote 10 minutes of time to this kind of listing. If buyers should show up whom they can't interest in any other piece of property, then they'll bring them to you in a last-chance effort at a commission. The opportunity to do work and not get paid for it is so great here that agents in general just don't want to bother with this type of listing.

About the only time it's used is in bare land, when the chances of selling are very slim and it could take years to produce a buyer. You might simply let every agent know that the property is for sale and you'll pay a commission, but you're not willing to give any one of them an "exclusive."

### Guaranteed-Sale Listing

A guaranteed-sale listing isn't a separate type of listing. Rather it's any of the above but is usually the exclusive right to sell. *The listing simply includes a separate clause which says that if the property isn't sold by the end of the listing term, then the agent agrees to buy it from you for a set price* (usually the listing price), less the commission.

Although widely used at one time, this type of listing is often frowned upon today because of the potential conflict of interest. The reason is simple. While an honest agent can use the guaranteed-sale listing to induce you to list, a dishonest agent can use it to gain a larger-than-expected commission.

A dishonest agent may induce an unwary seller to list, then take no action to sell the property. When the listing expires, the agent buys the house at a previously guaranteed low price and later resells at a much higher price. This is particularly a problem when the listing calls for the agent to buy the property for less than the listed price (justified by the supposed "fact" that because it didn't sell for the listed price, that price was too high).

If your agent suggests this type of listing, insist on the following (which may already be legally required in your state):

1. The agent can buy the property only for the listed price. No less.

2. The agent has to inform you, and you have to agree in writing to the price, if the agent resells the property to someone else within 1 year of your sale to the agent.

3. The agent must buy the property. The agent can't sell it to a third party in escrow, unless you get all the proceeds less the agreed-upon commission.

## Net Listing

The net listing is by far the most controversial type. *You agree up front on a fixed price for the property. Everything over that price goes to the agent.* You agree to sell for $100,000. If the agent brings in a buyer for $105,000, the agent gets $5000 as the commission. But if the agent brings in a buyer for $150,000 the agent gets $50,000 for a commission!

The opportunities to take advantage of a buyer here should be obvious. An unscrupulous agent could get a listing for a low price and then sell for a high one, getting an unconscionable commission.

A net listing is sometimes useful for a "hopeless" property. For one reason or another, the property isn't salable. So the buyer tells the agent, "Be creative. Find a buyer. Here's what I want. Everything else is yours."

In such an arrangement, you as the seller should insist (if state law doesn't already require it) that you be informed of the final selling price and that you agree in writing to it.

The easiest way to handle a net listing is to simply avoid it.

## Which Listing Should I Give?

The type of listing that's best for you depends, of course, on your situation and that of your property. It's a surprise to most sellers that in 95 percent of the cases, the listing that is likely to get you the best results is the exclusive right to sell.

In it you do give up your right to sell the property by yourself. But in exchange you get the best chance of having the agent put forth his or her best efforts in completing the sale.

If you give this type of listing, you want to be sure that your agent puts your house on a listing service (such as the Multiple Listing Service or whatever cooperative system is in use in your area). That guarantees that your house will get the widest possible exposure.

### TIP

In the trade, allowing other agents to work on a listing is called "cobroking" it. Be sure your agent agrees to cobroke your property with all other agents.

### TRAP

An old line that some agents use is to tell you, "To give you a better chance at a quick sale, I'll hold back the listing from the cooperative listing service for a few weeks. This means that all the agents in my office will work harder on it. It's really a better opportunity for you, the seller." Don't believe it. It's just a ploy to give the listing agent a chance to sell your property exclusively without having to split the commission. During those few weeks before your house gets on the cooperative system, your agent may indeed be knocking himself out trying to sell it. But that's one agent. On the service as many as 1000 or more agents will be aware that your house is for sale. One of them may already have a buyer looking for just what you've got.

Don't let the agent "vest pocket" your listing. Insist that it be given the widest possible exposure at the soonest possible time.

## Do You Understand the Listing Agreement?

The listing agreement is often several pages long and may contain a considerable amount of legalese. However, there are a number of points that it should contain and that you should watch out for.

### Items to Look for in a Listing Agreement

1. *Price.* The listing agreement should specify the price you expect to receive for your property.

2. *Deposit.* The agreement should indicate how large a deposit you expect from a buyer. It should also indicate that the agent may take the deposit, but that it is your money. Usually such agreements specify that if the buyer doesn't go through with the deal, you and the agent split the deposit.

3. *Terms.* It's important that the terms you are willing to accept are spelled out. For example, if you want only cash, your listing agreement should say that. If you are willing to accept a second mortgage as part of the purchase price, it should specify that as well. In actual practice, this doesn't preclude an agent from bringing you a buyer who offers other terms. It just means you don't have to accept such a buyer.

### TIP

It's important to be as specific as possible in the sales agreement, because once in a great while sellers may choose not to sell even though the agent has produced a buyer who is "ready, willing, and able" to purchase. In such a case, you could be liable for the commission even though you don't sell—unless the buyer doesn't meet the exact terms of the listing. Spelling out the terms can be very important.

4. *Title Insurance.* Today almost all property sold has title insurance. The only questions are which title company to use and who is going to pay for it. The listing agreement usually specifies both. In most areas title insurance costs are split between buyer and seller, although in some states the seller pays it. Find out what is commonly done in your area. Just be sure you don't pay for title insurance if you don't need too!

5. *Keybox.* Buyers come by when they're ready, not when you're ready. Therefore, it's a good idea to allow the agent to show the property even when you're not home. Since there may be many cooperative agents, the common way of handling this is to have a keybox installed. The listing agreement asks you to give permission for a keybox. Be aware, however, that you are opening your home up to a great many people.

### TRAP

Agents and buyers represent a broad spectrum of people. Just as in the general population, there are those who are scrupulously honest as well as those who are dishonest in real estate. While the incidence of theft from homes with lockboxes installed is small, it does occasionally occur. Therefore, for the time you have a lockbox on your home you are well advised to remove all valuables. *Note:* In many listing agreements the agents specifically disclaim responsibility for loss due to having a lockbox improperly used.

6. *Sign.* You should give permission for the agent to install a reasonable sign in your front yard. It's an excellent method of attracting buyers, perhaps the best.

7. *Arbitration and Attorney's Fees.* Typically these agreements call for arbitration in case of a dispute, and state that in the case of a lawsuit the prevailing party will have his or her attorney's costs paid by the losing party. Read this wording carefully. You may want to ask an attorney if you should sign or change it.

8. *Disclosure.* The listing agreement should also list the various disclosures that you as a seller must make to a buyer in your state. (These are handled in Chapter 17.)

9. *Equal Housing Disclosure.* You must be in compliance with federal and state antidiscrimination laws when you list your property.

10. *Beginning and Expiration Date.* Perhaps the most critical part of the document is the clause that states when the listing you are giving expires. It should be a written-out date—"June 1, 1997," not "in 3 months." If the date isn't inserted, the agent could insist that the listing you intended to be for 3 months is actually for much longer.

### TIP

I suggest never giving a listing for more than 3 months. In most markets that should be enough time for a good agent to find a buyer. If there are extenuating circumstances, at the end of the 3-month period, you might want to extend the listing for an additional 3 months. Or you might want to secure the services of a different agent.

### TRAP

Beware of the agent who insists on a long listing. This could be a "lister," an agent who simply takes listings and lets them sit. Giving a longer listing might mean it will take longer to sell your house. My feeling is that no really good agent will normally want more than 3 months to sell a house in a stable market. After that, if the house doesn't sell, it could be overpriced or there could be some problem with it that will keep it from selling indefinitely—and it might not be worth the agent's time to bother with it. Wanting a long-term listing is a danger signal.

11. *Commission.* The agreement will state the percentage of commission that you've agreed upon. Beware of a clause right next to it which may state something to the effect that if you take your house off the market for any reason, you owe the agent a fee that is then written in. This is a "liquidated damages" clause and it means that although you may not have to pay the full commission if you decide not to sell, you are committing yourself to paying something, often a substantial amount of money. Have your attorney check this out.

In addition to the listing agreement itself, most agents will provide you with an agent's disclosure document stating whether the agent is a seller's, buyer's, or dual agent. Recheck Chapter 3 if you're not sure about this.

## What Are the Danger Signals with Regard to Listings?

1. Long-term listings.
2. Very high commissions.
3. Pressure on you to sign. If brokers pressure you to sign the listing, think what they'll do when a bad offer comes in.
4. Lister willing to accept any sales price on the listing, even though you know it's too high. The lister just wants you to sign and hope that after a month or so when you can't sell, you'll drop your price.
5. Hedging on the disclosures, saying that you can trust them to look out for your interests.
6. Insisting on a listing (net or guaranteed sale) that allows them to make a higher commission without letting you know that they need your written permission.
7. Wanting your power of attorney to sign a deal. If you give up your power of attorney, the agent could accept an offer for you that you really don't want.

# 6

# How to Get Your Agent to Work Harder

You sign a listing agreement with an agent in which you commit to paying that agent a large commission for bringing you a buyer. What does that agent commit to you in return? What is the agent bound to do?

In most cases, questions of this sort arise after the home has been listed for a couple of months. With few to no buyers coming by, you're getting anxious. You're beginning to wonder if you chose the right agent after all. You look in the paper and you don't see your home advertised. Your agent isn't holding an "open house" in your home. What's he or she doing? Your question is born out of frustration.

Your next question is probably: What is the agent supposed to be doing? Is she not living up to her responsibilities and duties? Your final question is likely to be: What can I do about it? We'll deal with these questions in this chapter.

## What Is Your Agent Supposed to Do for You?

Basically, your agent is supposed to sell your home. How he or she does that, in general, is up to the agent. Advertising your property and holding "open houses" in it, per se, are no guarantee of buyers.

**TIP**

Studies have repeatedly shown that buyers rarely purchase the home they call about on an advertisement or
visit on an open house. Just because agents don't advertise your property or hold an open house in your home
doesn't, of itself, mean they aren't working hard.

Some sellers insist on writing into their listing agreements that
the agent will spend X dollars on advertising. The hope is that if
the agent commits to a large enough figure for advertising the
property, then he or she will push the property.

Maybe that works and maybe not. Most good agents I know
won't agree to a set advertising figure. They know that it's money
just wasted and it reduces their commission. In the end, the agent
who agrees to spending a set figure on advertising may not be the
best agent to sell your property.

## What Can Your Agent Do for You?

The part that the agent can do best—talking up your home to
other agents who might potentially have buyers—you will never
get a chance to see. Consider how the "system" works. You list your
home with one of possibly thousands of agents in your area. On
the other side of the fence, the vast majority of buyers seek out
agents to find the right home for them. They know that the great
preponderance of homes also are listed. Therefore, it only makes
sense to look with the aid of an agent.

You're listed with an agent; potential buyers are looking with
agents. All that's needed is for your agent to contact the right
buyer's agent and a deal can be made.

Listing books help. They usually show a picture of your house
and give a description. But there may be dozens, even hundreds,
of homes in your price range.

What makes your home stand out from all the others? What your
agent can do for you is to "talk up" your house to other agents. He
can stand up at a listing meeting (attended by many agents from
different offices) and say, "I've got a house here that will knock
your socks off. And my seller has reduced the price (if indeed you

have)." Or the agent can say, "This home has the best view in the area." Or, "It offers terrific terms." Or, "My seller has said, bring me any reasonable offer!" (You surely did say that, didn't you?)

You get the idea. Your agent's best weapon is spreading the word around, and anything you can do to help your agent accomplish that (such as reduce the price, offer better terms, or make your home "show" beautifully) only helps.

### TIP

A good agent has an ethical responsibility to keep you informed at all times. That means that the agent calls you weekly to let you know what he or she has done to sell your home. This is not only good business practice, but it also may help with the sale, since during those conversations you may be able to suggest sales approaches that the agent didn't think of. If your agent doesn't call you frequently, call your agent and demand to know what's going on.

## What Can You Do if Your Agent Isn't Working for You?

This question almost never arises until at least after the first month and usually during the second month of the listing. Until then, most sellers are filled with hope, even if no one comes by to see the house.

However, if the agent doesn't call, no buyers come by, there are no ads in the paper, and time is going by, you are very likely to get frustrated and angry. About this time most sellers call that darn agent and give him a piece of their mind.

Calling accomplishes two things. It makes the seller feel temporarily better, and it makes the agent angry and even less likely to work hard on the sale of the house. Thus, yelling at your agent can be counterproductive.

### But What Can You Do?

Determine if your agent really isn't working. Call or go to see your agent and instead of showing anger, show concern. Explain that you haven't seen any results and, after all, results are what listing and selling is all about. Give the agent an opportunity to explain and listen carefully to the explanation.

Does it make sense? Has the agent talked up your house all over town? Was the agent just too busy to call you and let you know? Has a plan been put into effect to sell your property?

Remember, a good agent will always find time to call and keep you informed. It would take an extraordinary set of circumstances to keep a good agent from not talking to you. (But then again, the extraordinary happens every day in our world.)

Give the agent a second chance. If you are near the beginning or middle of the listing period, give the agent another 2 weeks. See what happens.

If after a second chance, the agent still refuses to work on your property, and you have only a few more weeks left on the listing, common sense suggests that you wait it out. The listing will soon expire and you can go elsewhere. On the other hand, if you've signed a long-term listing, you can only demand to have your listing back. Say you're unsatisfied with the agent's work and you want to list it elsewhere.

**TRAP**

When you sign a listing for a set period of time, generally speaking you cannot take back your listing unless the agent agrees. Some listing agreements contain a "liquidated damages" clause. Beware of this clause. It states that if for any reason you decide to take your house off the market, you owe the agent whatever fee was written in there.

## How Do I Get My Listing Back?

There are many reasons that sellers want to get out of the listing. Perhaps they have found someone they can sell the house to without the agent, and they want to avoid paying a commission. Or perhaps they've had an offer to rent the property. Or maybe the sellers are convinced the agent just isn't doing a good job.

These are all common reasons. However, when a seller hires an agent and agrees to an exclusive right-to-sell listing (the most common kind), the seller gives up the right to sell or lease during the listing period without the agent's consent. Quite frankly, if the seller insists on breaking the agreement, the agent is entitled to a part if not all of the commission.

### Give an Acceptable Reason

On the other hand, there are other reasons for wanting to get out of a listing that the agent may readily accept. The seller or a member of the immediate family may have become ill, the seller could have lost his or her job, the house could have partly burned down. These are all excellent reasons for getting out of a listing and, in most cases, the agent will readily agree. (If the agent refuses, go to the local real estate board—it should be sympathetic and should apply pressure on the agent.)

### Judgment Calls for Breaking the Listing

Then there is the middle ground. This is when you, the seller, feel the agent hasn't done any work and hasn't lived up to the listing agreement. The last time you saw or heard from the agent was when you signed the listing. There has been no sign in the yard and no advertising, and as far as you can tell, the agent hasn't talked up your property. (Maybe the agent even left on vacation as soon as you signed up!) Your house isn't selling while others are. No potential buyers are coming by. You want out, either so you can try selling it yourself or so you can get a different agent.

When you finally get hold of your agent, she says that she has worked on your listing as hard as possible, and she refuses to give it up.

If you take this to the local real estate board, you're unlikely to get a sympathetic hearing. After all, who really is to say what constitutes working with diligence on a listing? Therefore, what can you do to get out of your listing?

## How to Put Pressure on Your
## Agent to Release Your Listing

1. If your agent is a salesperson, tell him that you are going to complain to the broker. If this doesn't do any good, go to see the broker and state your case. The broker may or may not be sympathetic, depending on whether that broker thinks you are justified in your thinking.

2. Tell your agent that you are quite angry and that you are going to file a written complaint with the local real estate board and the state real estate licensing department. Quite frankly, since it's a matter of judgment, neither of these steps is likely to produce much in the way of results. But most agents would rather not have letters of complaint registered against them. Show the agent the letters. If this doesn't move the agent, send the letters on with a copy to the agent.

3. Tell the agent you're going to complain in writing to the local chamber of commerce, better business bureau, or even the district attorney. Show the letters to the agent before sending them. If the agent doesn't become agreeable to what you want, send the letters. Again, since it's a judgment call, don't expect big results.

4. Tell your agent you're going to write a letter of complaint to your local newspaper. This is a no-win situation for the agent. There's always a chance your letter of complaint will end up in the letters-to-the-editor department. That will draw public attention to the problem—a powerful tactic. If you've already said you were going to send letters (as described above) and then did, the agent will surely believe that you'll send this one. And who knows what letters local newspapers (which are traditionally hungry for any news at all to fill their pages) will print. If the agent doesn't go along, send the letter—just be sure that your letter states facts and does *not* contain any slander or libelous statements.

Notice that all of the above tactics have two parts. First you tell the agent what you are going to do and give him a chance to respond. If he doesn't agree to give you back your listing, then you do it. The steps also follow in sequence from lesser to greater pressure.

The point is that in reality, there's probably nothing specific that you can do. All that you can hope for is to convince the agent that you're sufficiently mad about what the agent has (or has not) done and that it's easier and better just to give back the listing. After a while you become a nuisance, and just to get rid of your complaining, the agent may give you back your listing.

What happens if your agent is a real stinker and isn't moved by any of it?

Hopefully you didn't sign a really long listing and by the time you try all of the above maneuvers, the listing period will almost be up anyway. Just wait it out and get a better agent.

# 7

# Selling Successfully on Your Own (FSBO)

Each year, more than 10 percent of homes are sold by owners without going through an agent. These sellers either save money on the commission they would otherwise pay or get a faster sale by lowering their price—or both. You can be among their number.

Selling FSBO (for sale by owner), however, takes a certain mindset that not everyone has. It also takes patience and effort. It would be a mistake to think that all you need do is put a sign in the front yard and wait for buyers to hand you a deposit. To sell FSBO, you're going to have to do much of the work that an agent does—in some ways more. Of course, the results can be quite rewarding.

In this chapter we're going to see what's involved in a FSBO sale and how to get started pulling it off successfully.

## Are Market Conditions Right for Doing an FSBO?

FSBOs are most easily done in strong markets. If you're in a hot or seller's market, your chances of selling by owner are dramatically increased. After all, if there are more buyers than sellers, it only stands to reason that it's easier to make a sale, and save a commission.

However, FSBOs also do well in very weak markets. Here the key is offering a lower price than your competitors (other home sellers). Consider that if your neighbor is selling her home for $100,000 and paying a 6 percent commission, she's actually receiving $94,000 net after the agent's fee.

You, however, by selling direct, can offer the buyer a $94,000 price (because there is no agent) and still get the same net as your neighbor. Now, if you were a buyer, which house would you pick first—the one costing $100,000 (your neighbor's) or the one costing $94,000 (yours)? In essence, by giving to the buyer the commission you would otherwise pay to an agent, you get a faster sale.

## Do You Have the Necessary Experience?

If you haven't ever sold a home before (by going through an agent), then I would discourage you from trying to sell on your own the first time out. Just as with doing your own taxes, it's better if you have an expert do it the first time. That way you can see how a deal is handled and get a feel for the steps involved. That doesn't mean that you can't do it the first time you try. It just means that the chances of your getting yourself in trouble or ruining what otherwise would be a good deal are too great to warrant doing it.

## Are You Prepared to Deal Directly with Buyers?

If you do decide to move forward, keep in mind that you will be on the front line in dealing with buyers. Yes, we're all people, and buyers are just nice people looking for a home. But the moment they become potential buyers for your home, they also become adversaries. Their goals are exactly the opposite of yours. They are trying to get the price down; you want to keep it up. They want you to throw in the refrigerator, the furniture, maybe even the cat. You want to take everything with you. They want you to finance the house at 3 percent interest. You want them to get their own loan or pay you 20 percent interest.

When dealing with buyers, you're going to have to be prepared to tackle an often aggressive adversary, all the while putting on a smile and keeping a cheerful outlook. The buyers are going to make you sweat, make you worry, even make you fearful. Are you ready to cope with that?

## Can You Handle the Paperwork?

In the old days you just found a buyer, took a deposit, and opened escrow. That was about it, except for the signing of documents and the receipt of your check. Today, however, things are different. There are long sales agreements that almost require a lawyer's discerning eye to analyze. There are implied warranties, disclosure statements, inspections, and much more. All of these are normally handled by an agent. But now, you'll have to handle them yourself. (Or, as we'll see shortly, hire someone competent to handle them for you.) Are you willing to go the extra distance this requires?

## Are You Willing to Give Up Weekends and Evenings?

Buyers don't do anything for your convenience. They do everything for their own. They figure that if they're going to spend $100,000, more or less, on a house, then you, the seller, had better cater to them. That means that you have to be ready to show the place at the drop of hat. A couple drives by, sees your home, and calls. But, you tell them, you haven't dressed, you haven't cleaned the house, and you've got a terrible headache.

Okay, they say, there are other houses to see and plenty of agents who'll show them. *Damn*, you think, and let them in. Are you prepared for that? (Actually, it's not that bad—and you have to be prepared to show your property at a moment's notice even if you work through an agent.)

## Can You Help a Buyer with Financing Questions?

Nobody pays cash. Financing is part and parcel of every deal. You can't get a sale without a loan.

The trouble is, most buyers don't know a thing about financing. They're counting on the agent to help them. But with no agent, there's only you. Are you up to it? (Actually, these days it sounds far more difficult than it really is. You can contact a mortgage broker early on, and he or she can usually field all the buyer's financing questions for you.)

So you see, selling a home FSBO isn't as easy as it sounds—or as difficult. But it is trickier than simply signing on with an agent.

If your appetite for doing it yourself is still whetted, then read on. Here's how you can get started.

## How Do I Get the Word Out About My FSBO?

When you sell by yourself, you must do everything in your power to let people know your home is for sale. That includes giving flyers to neighbors (and making them available in a little box on your sign), putting up notices on bulletin boards, contacting any nearby housing offices of major companies, even going on-line and leaving messages on electronic bulletin boards. It also includes paying for newspaper advertising. Here are some tips on that most expensive of venues.

In newspaper advertising (as elsewhere), less is more. The classic mistake that novice sellers make is saying too much in the ad (and paying too much for it as well). I've seen sellers take out full-column, even double-column, ads for their home—unnecessarily spending hundreds of dollars. Perhaps they are hoping to compete with agents' ads.

### TRAP

One of the biggest misunderstandings that all sellers have is to think that a buyer who sees their ad in the paper is likely to come out and buy their house. Buyers rarely buy homes they see advertised.

Real estate agents put ads in the paper for two reasons, in addition to attracting buyers: to appease sellers and make them believe the agent is working hard, and to get listings! Agents know that callers on ads often have their own property to sell. They hope to sign them up. An FSBO seller, on the other hand, has only one home to sell. You can't sign up a listing, and most of the time the buyers who come over will be disappointed with the home and won't buy.

Don't get discouraged, play the odds. Get enough
potential buyers through that front door and one of
them will make an offer.

Of course, agents are trying to lure in buyers and sellers for many
different properties as well as to get listings; you have only one home
and aren't interested in listings. Hence, you shouldn't—really
can't—compete with them. On the other hand, you have a big lure
that you can put in your ad that agents can't: the letters FSBO.
Would-be buyers love to check out FSBOs (because they smell a deal
and know that agents aren't likely to show them these properties).

Therefore, with FSBO (or "By Owner") leading off your ad, you
can be well on the way to attracting buyers.

## Items to Include
## in an FSBO Ad

1. Indicate you're selling FSBO or "By Owner."
2. Give the style of the home and the neighborhood locations (but
   not the address, for security reasons); include any special features.
3. Give the number of bedrooms and baths in the house.
4. Give the price.
5. Give the general condition of the property.
6. Give your phone number or a number where you can be reached.

Here's a typical ad from a newspaper:

BY OWNER

In Maple Schools
Large 4 bed, 3 bath
Newly painted, pool, spa
Must sell $135,000 555-2134

This newspaper ad is lean and mean. There are few extraneous
words. And it cuts right to the chase with "must sell" and the price.
Presumably any buyer interested in the price range, location, and
schools will find the ad enticing—and will call.

Would a bigger ad be better? Many advertising specialists say bigger is better because it's easier to see. However, in the case of homes for sale, buyers usually are meticulous in going down a long list of tiny ads looking for bargains, so the cost of a big ad might just be wasted. In addition, a bigger ad might just show how inexperienced you really are at selling a home. Finally, anything else you might add at this point might just as likely scare away as many buyers as it attracts. For example, you list that the home has a dog runway. There might be more buyers who don't have dogs and don't want runs than do.

If you still feel uncomfortable in designing an ad, check out your local library or bookstore. There are at least a dozen good books on designing advertising that gets results. Take one out and follow its advice.

## What About a Sign?

A sign is a must. It doesn't have to be elaborate. But it should be large enough to be easily seen by motorists passing by and it should look good. You can find ready-made FSBO signs at stationery stores for just a few dollars, but I suggest popping for the $50 or so it costs to have one made up just for you. After all, you're talking about saving a commission worth thousands; surely you can afford a sign worth a few bucks! When you get the sign, plant it firmly in the lawn where it can most easily be seen by people passing in cars. This isn't necessarily in the center of your front yard. It could be off to the side or even attached to a tree or fence.

Don't forget to put your phone number on the sign. Some sellers also add, "BY APPOINTMENT ONLY." That doesn't mean that a potential buyer won't come rapping at your door, but it tends to suggest to most that a call first might be in order.

### TRAP

Some locales have sign ordinances. These may restrict the number of signs you can use, their size, or even whether you're allowed to put a sign out at all. Check with your local building department or homeowners' association if you have any questions here.

## Do I Have to Show the Property?

Of course you do. Who else is there?

There are several concerns here, the biggest of which usually is security. You're letting people into your house without really knowing who they are or what their ulterior motives might be. For some sellers this is no problem. For others, it's a big concern. If it concerns you, get an agent who can screen people before he or she brings them by. There's really no other good solution.

**TIP**

Some FSBO sellers concerned with security require potential buyers to call first and won't show the property until they get the full name, phone number, and address of the buyer. Then they call the buyer back. At least that tends to confirm that buyers have their own place and are somewhat established. On the other hand, it can insult some buyers and cause them not to come by.

When you do show the property, warmly welcome the prospective buyers and point out a few of the amenities of the house. After you've talked for a few moments, allow the buyers to wander through the property themselves. (They need to be able to feel that it's their own house.)

**TRAP**

Put away any valuables in your rooms. You never know who's honest and who's a thief. Buyers wandering through might just slip a necklace or watch into their pocket and be gone. (You should do the same even if the house is listed with an agent.)

**TIP**

Take a photo of your house (one view of the front, another inside) and make a list of all its features. Get this copied at a local copy shop, including a map showing exactly where your house is located. Be sure your name and phone number are included. Give everyone who comes by a copy. A buyer may want to come back later and not be able to find the property, or may want to call you and not have your phone number. This is an excellent method of recalling both.

**TIP**

Have a "guest book" located conveniently near the front door. Ask potential buyers to sign their names and give their phone numbers. This gives you a record of who came through so you can call people back. Later, if you subsequently list with an agent, you can exclude those people and need not pay a commission if they buy.

## How Do I Handle the Documents?

There are a large number of documents that are involved in the sale of your house. These include:

The sales agreement (deposit receipt)

Disclosure forms

Escrow instructions

Termite and other clearances

Deeds

And yet more. If you're like most people, you will find these documents to be arcane and forbidding. Do you have the right ones? Are they filled out properly? Is something or some document missing?

My advice is, don't try to fill out any of the sales documents without the aid of a good attorney or a competent agent. Selling a house involves legally binding actions. If you fill out a document incorrectly and later on, trouble results, you can't simply say that you didn't know. You should have known.

### How Do I Get a Professional to Help with the Paperwork?

There are several possibilities:

1. Hire a real estate agent for a set fee to do this task. As noted at the beginning, some agents are willing to do the paperwork. (Today, fewer agents will take on the job because of the potential liability.)

2. Hire a real estate attorney. Chances are you're going to need one sooner or later in the transaction. Hire an attorney right at the beginning to draft all documents.

**TRAP**

If you hire an attorney, be sure that he or she is a *real estate* specialist. Most attorneys aren't, and they can muck up a deal by knowing enough generally but not enough specifically about how to handle the transaction.

3. If you know a good escrow officer, get him to handle some of the documents for you. Be aware, however, that escrow officers are not real estate agents or lawyers. Their knowledge could be limited in critical areas. You might want to have an agent or attorney handle the deposit receipt and disclosures and the escrow officer handle the remaining paperwork.

## What About the Financing?

As noted earlier, the vast majority of buyers do not pay cash. They expect to get a mortgage or trust deed for 80 percent or more of the purchase price. Thus, one of the biggest problems that you face when selling your own property is how to help the buyer arrange the financing. On the surface, this can seem an insurmountable problem. Once tackled directly, however, it's not really all that difficult (provided you're not going to try any "fancy" or creative financing).

Essentially you need to be able to tell the buyers that you have talked to some lenders and that you have determined that a new first mortgage on your property is obtainable. All they have to do is contact the lenders themselves. (It's what often happens, even if they deal with an agent.) This way the buyers are not left out in the cold and on their own.

What you need to do is to contact a couple of banks, savings and loans, or mortgage bankers. Talk to the lending officers and find out their procedures for handling financing. Get their charges and fees and prepare a short "shopping list." Update it at least weekly. Your list should include:

Name of lender and contact person

Maximum loan amounts

Points charged (each point equals 1 percent of the loan)

Other fees for the loan

Now, when buyers seem interested, you can hand them the list and suggest they contact one of the lenders. If the buyers are "first-timers," you may even want to go with them to the lender to smooth out any rough spots (although most buyers prefer to keep their personal finances private).

## How Do I Set Up an Escrow?

What could be simpler? After a buyer has signed a sales agreement to purchase your home, just take the document down to a local escrow company. Any escrow company will take it from there.

### TRAP

Don't expect advice, or at least good advice, from every escrow officer. Escrow companies are neutral third parties. In most cases, they know their job fairly well. They'll prepare all the necessary documents to close the deal and they'll tell you what actions, documents, or monies have to be deposited to escrow in order to make the deal. But don't expect your escrow officer to answer questions such as, "Which termite inspection company should I use?" Or, "The buyer wants me to repaint the interior, but I don't want to—how do we resolve this?"

Those are problems you'll have to resolve with the buyer.

### TIP

Very often the various people involved in the sale will provide the necessary information and direction to help with closing. The loan officer, for example, will often help the buyer straighten out credit problems. The real estate attorney will help you clear up title problems. The escrow officer will provide the document for a second mortgage, if you need it. And so forth.

## Avoiding Potential Problems

In truth, in most cases, once you have found buyers who have signed a purchase agreement, the remainder of the transaction should progress smoothly. You should have few problems, assuming you know the basics of a sale.

However, in some cases problems arise. These can take many forms.

### Potential Problems

- Disputes with the buyer
- Serious title problems
- The buyer's inability or lack of desire to perform
- A sudden increase in interest rates, keeping the buyer from qualifying
- A physical problem with your house
- Problems with local government bodies such as the building department or planning commission

It's at this point that you may very well need expert help. Your real estate attorney can provide some of it, particularly in matters of legality. But in matters of common sense and in disputes, your best ally is a real estate agent. You may need to bring an agent in for either a fixed fee or a percentage of the sale. (Of course, if you already have a buyer, you wouldn't expect to pay the agent a full commission.)

## Making the Big "FSBO" Decision

These, then, are your many potential problems as well as your options. Should you hire an agent? Or should you try to sell by yourself?

Try this decision sheet to help you make up your mind.

### FSBO Decision Sheet

1. What's the condition of the housing market in your area?

|  |  |
|---|---|
| Hot | [ ] |
| Warm | [ ] |
| Cool | [ ] |
| Cold | [ ] |

|  | YES | NO |
|---|---|---|
| 2. Are you clear on the steps to selling a home? | [ ] | [ ] |
| 3. Are you up to date on the disclosure requirements, needed documents, and real estate law in your area? | [ ] | [ ] |
| 4. Are you okay with handling people looking through your home? | [ ] | [ ] |
| 5. Are you agreeable to letting strangers enter your home? | [ ] | [ ] |
| 6. Will you give up your weekends and evenings to show your home to potential buyers? | [ ] | [ ] |
| 7. Do you have a plan for handling the sales agreement, and who will fill it out? | [ ] | [ ] |
| 8. Do you have a plan for handling disputes with the buyer both before an offer is presented and afterward? | [ ] | [ ] |
| 9. Have you worked out the financing so that you can give the buyer options? | [ ] | [ ] |

|  | YES | NO |
|---|---|---|

10. Have you contacted an escrow company, a real estate attorney, and an agent, and has each agreed to handle a specific part of the deal?                        [ ]          [ ]

11. Have you readied an ad and are you willing to stick a " For Sale by Owner" sign in your front yard?                  [ ]          [ ]

The more yes answers, the more likely it is that you'll be able to successfully sell your property on your own. Before you ultimately decide, however, here's one last bit of advice. Remember that regardless of how high a real estate agent's fee may be, the agent performs a service: he or she earns that money. If you don't use the agent, you'll have to do the work yourself.

### TIP

One compromise that many successful FSBO sellers use is to set a time limit for selling by themselves. They will try being a FSBO, for example, for 1 month or 3 months. If, during that time, they haven't sold the property, they will then list with an agent.

This is an excellent plan. It allows you to try to sell it yourself and it assures you that later on you won't feel that you could have done it, if only you'd tried. I would only caution that you set a realistic time limit. The time period doesn't matter, as long as you aren't in a rush to sell.

If you sell, great. But after some point, if you still haven't sold the house, you should agree in your own mind that you'll try an agent. Otherwise, you could be spending a very long and frustrating time without any accomplishment to show for it.

My book *For Sale by Owner* (1995) offers more information on successfully selling your home.

# 8
# Quick Fixes to Make Your Home More Salable

The most important factor in getting buyers to like a house is how well it "shows." (If buyers don't *like* the property, they're unlikely to make an offer, almost no matter how good a deal it is.) Houses that show well, sell. Houses that don't are called "dogs" in the trade. If you have a dog, you aren't going to sell quickly or for the price you want. However, you can usually turn that dog into a good-looking home without that much effort or expense. We'll see how in this chapter.

## Why Is "Curb Appeal" So Important?

We've all heard the adage, "You never have a second chance to make a good first impression." The point is well taken. Attitudes toward people and homes are usually fixed and sometimes unchangeable with that first glance. With regard to homes, that first impression is called "curb appeal." It means how well your home shows itself off when that potential buyer drives up the very first time. There are several elements that go into curb appeal.

### Elements of Curb Appeal

- Overall neighborhood
- Location on block
- Condition of landscaping

- Overall look of home
- Appearance of details (driveway, entranceway, front door, and so on)

Some things you can do a lot about; others are basically out of your hands. As noted in Chapter 1, there are only a few limited ways you can improve your neighborhood. And how your home sets on the block is pretty much locked in. (You can plant or cut back shrubs to give your home a better drive-up look.)

On the other hand, you can do a lot with landscaping and the appearance of your home, including the details. To recap Chapter 1, here is a list of must-do items if you're serious about selling your property.

**Must-Do Fix-Up Work**

1. Fix the driveway.
2. Manicure front lawns and shrubs.
3. Paint the front.
4. Repaint or replace the front door.

All of the above are inexpensive, particularly if you do the work yourself. Once it is done, you will have enormously increased the curb appeal of your home. Don't do the work and you may hear potential buyers softly barking as they drive by your place.

## What If My House Is Already in Pretty Good Shape?

Beyond the "must-dos" noted above, if your home is already in pretty good shape you probably can get by with little other fix-up work. However, be sure that what you see as "pretty good shape" is what a potential buyer will see as "good shape" too.

- Pretty good shape usually means that the paint looks good on the outside (no blisters peeling, or fading ) and inside (no marks or scratches).
- It means that the lawns around the property don't have bald spots and aren't overgrown with weeds, and that the house has hedges and trees and decent landscaping everywhere.

■ It means that all the appliances work.

If your house is in pretty good shape, what you should do is launch a major *clean-up* effort. If you've lived in your present home for more than 6 months, chances are you've got a couple of loads of trash and throwaways stashed here and there that you would do well to throw away.

### TIP

Remember to clean out the furniture in your home! What you see as "cozy" most buyers will see as cluttered. The rule of thumb is, get rid of half your furniture (store it, sell it, dump it) and buyers will think your home is just right.

When you're thinning out your furniture, here's a list to help you along.

### Get Rid Of

1. Extra furniture. One double/queen in a bedroom is maximum. One table and set of chairs in a dining room. No cluttered chairs or couches in living or family room. No rugs on top of rugs.
2. Any clothes that are not in drawers or *neatly* hung in closets.
3. Any toys scattered on the floor and not neatly put away in drawers or boxes.
4. Any items that would get in the way of a buyer's appreciation of the house.

### Clean Up

1. The kitchen. *Never, never* leave dirty dishes out. Nothing turns buyers off more.
2. The carpets. People look down, and the first thing that buyers look at once inside are the carpets. Clean carpets make a positive impression. New carpets make a much better one. (Even inexpensive brand-new carpets look great.)

3. The drapes. They're the next thing that buyers look at.

4. Smudges or spots on walls. Most can be wiped off with detergent and a sponge. Otherwise, paint the wall.

5. Junk and trash in the front, back, or side yards. Haul it away. You're going to have to move it as soon as you sell anyhow.

6. Windows. Buyers like to be able to see out. Clean or replace old screens too.

These are things you can do if your home is already in pretty good shape. Now let's consider a home in not so good shape.

## What If My Home Is in Bad Shape?

You have to make the decision "if it's worth it" to do the cleaning and repairing. Remember, however, that most of the repair work is not that expensive, if you do the labor yourself.

### TRAP

If you don't do needed repair and cleanup work, buyers will begin characterizing your property as a "fixer-upper" and will submit lowball offers. Buyers always exaggerate the cost of fixing up a property.

The following list describes the most common major fix-ups as well as tips on how to handle them.

### Fix It Up

1. *Roof.*   Sometimes you can simply fix an old roof where it's leaking and not replace it. The cost is far, far less.

2. *Insulation.*   Older homes do not have much insulation, but today's buyers are keen on energy efficiency and will sometimes turn down a property just because it lacks adequate insulation. The cost for adding blown-in insulation to an attic is low. To add insulation to walls on an already constructed house, however, is enormously costly and should be avoided if at all possible.

3. *Electrical and plumbing.* You'll need to bring electricity and pipes up to minimal safety standards in any event. In most cases, the work needed to be done is minimal. On the other hand, if you have to convert galvanized steel pipes to copper pipes, be prepared for a major blow to your wallet.

4. *Walls.* External stucco should be patched, unless it's so badly broken up that it has to be totally replaced. Patching is cheap; replacement is very expensive. Interior wallboard should be patched where there are holes. You can do this yourself for next to nothing.

5. *Garage door.* New hinges and springs are a good idea for safety reasons, and are inexpensive. Most wooden doors can be repaired inexpensively. Metal doors may have to be replaced.

6. *Landscaping.* If you put in a new lawn by sod, it costs more, but is instantly green. Seeds take up to 3 months to produce lush grass but cost pennies per foot. Forget about adding shade trees. They need years to grow, and planting already large trees is costly. Flower beds, however, are inexpensive and add color and vitality to landscaping. Also, fix the fence if it's falling down. Buyers start adding up costs when they see a broken fence.

7. *Built-in appliances.* Broken appliances should be fixed or replaced. Sometimes it's cheaper to replace than to fix. For example, an entire electric range and oven may cost under $400, while a single burner (there are usually five to seven on the unit, including oven) could cost $100.

There could, of course, be other areas requiring major repair. In all cases you should get bids as well as competitively price materials yourself to determine whether you'll get your money for repair work out from the sale and/or whether doing so will help you sell faster.

## What If My Property Is a Real Dog?

Many people have never seen a house in truly terrible condition. Typically it results from absentee owners who rent the place out to tenants who just don't care. For many readers, the following list will just make them feel good about their own property. Here are some things that could be wrong with a property that would make your hair stand on end.

### Problems with a House in Terrible Condition

Appliances—ripped apart, stolen, or smashed

Bathroom fixtures—ripped off walls or out of floors and broken

Light fixtures—stolen or smashed (including the electrical receptacle)

Windows—broken

Doors—broken

Screens—gone

Plumbing—broken lines

Electrical—main circuit box smashed, circuit breakers broken, wiring pulled out

Walls and ceiling—major holes

Yard—no landscaping; weeds, rocks, and dirt

Fence—broken

Exterior—stucco falling apart, wood torn off or scratched, metal siding bent or broken loose

Ridiculous, you may say? A house could never get that bad? I've seen them that bad and worse. But being in terrible shape doesn't mean the house is valueless. The condition just means that you have to decide on a plan of action.
You have several choices:

1. Fix it up completely.
2. Fix it up for safety and cosmetic effect.
3. Let it alone and sell it as a fixer-upper for much less.

## Buyers Have No Imagination

At this point you have to realize that buyers ordinarily suffer from an appalling lack of imagination. If you have a house that is a real dog and you're fortunate enough to get a buyer to walk into the front door, chances are 99 out of 100 the buyer will immediately turn around and walk out. The vast majority of buyers, even investor/buyers, won't want to fool around with a real dog *even if the price is cut-rate.*

That means that in order to sell the property, you're probably going to have to do some work. You fix it up either totally or just cosmetically (enough to sell).

### TIP

It's going to cost big bucks to fix up a real dog of a house, so you should consider short-term financing in the form of a homeowner's loan or a home equity loan. In many cases, the interest on such a loan is tax deductible, as are *many* of your fix-up expenses. Check with your accountant.

Should you fix up a dog of a house?

You simply have to do a cost/reward analysis. In a strong market and in a good area, the answer is undoubtedly yes. However, in a bad market and in a terrible neighborhood, maybe the best you can do is slap some paint on and hope for the best.

### TRAP

Cosmetic repair does not mean leaving health and safety problems undone. In order to sell in most areas of the country today, the house must be up to at least minimal building and safety standards.

## Do I Have the Energy?

Then, there's the matter of how much energy you are willing (or have) to devote to the fix-up. Some of us are natural putterers. Fixing up a place for us is fun.

For most of the rest of us, however, fun is playing golf, watching TV, or reading a good book. And then there are those who have two left hands and who wouldn't think of trying to do fix-up themselves. Where do you fit in? (It's important to know, because if you have to hire everything out, it could be prohibitively expensive.)

Here's my suggestion. If you don't want to (or can't) spend a lot of energy yourself fixing up your home before you sell, forget it. Pay someone else to do what's minimally necessary to cosmetically clean and paint your property. Then take the lower price and wait the longer time to find a buyer. (Sometimes it's more important to cater to yourself than to cater to your house.)

On the other hand, if you're a bundle of energy, then by all means leap into the fray and fix up your house yourself. Try to do much of the work yourself, since that's actually the best way to save money.

### TIP

In a hot market, buyers tend to overlook more about a house's condition. Yes, if it's in terrible shape they will either not buy or knock the price down. But if it's in "okay" shape, chances are they won't complain that much. In a *hot* market it's hard enough just finding a house to buy in a price range a buyer can afford, let alone worrying about the small stuff.

### TRAP

Many sellers fall into the trap of thinking that by doing *excessive* fix-up work on their house, they can make *even more* money from the sale. Chances are that just isn't so. Your property will have a top market value beyond which it just won't go at the present time. What you do when you fix it up is to try to present it in such as way as to get that top dollar. You do the *minimal amount of fix-up possible.* Any additional fixing could turn your property into a white elephant, overbuilt for its neighborhood.

My book *The Home Remodeling Organizer* (1995) offers more information on fixing up your home for sale.

# 9

# Counteroffering the Buyer

It's what you've been waiting for since you first decided to put your home on the market. All those weekends of painting and fixing up, those hours of research finding the right price to ask, the talking and interviewing until you came up with just the right agent (or decided to sell FSBO)—they've all paid off. You've finally got an offer!

You got a call. There's an offer on your home. An agent is going to bring it by in just a short while.

Hooray! You're finally on your way out of this house and on with your life. You can hardly wait. At last it's over. The long ordeal has ended.

Wrong!

If you're like most sellers, your ordeal has just begun. For when that agent or buyer comes over and you take a look at that offer, you'd better be sitting down. Unless you're in a hot market, the offer is likely to be for a price much lower than you want to accept and the terms are very likely to be onerous to you. In other words, the offer has every chance of being unacceptable.

Now, the real process of selling your house begins. You have to negotiate with the buyers in the hopes that you can get at least what you feel you minimally need and they, hopefully, will still want to purchase.

Negotiations with counteroffers flying back and forth often take a long time and can stretch into the wee hours of the morning. I've heard many sellers complain that the negotiations were the hardest, the most painful part of the entire sales procedure. One even moaned that it was worse than getting a tooth filled without anesthetic!

Our goal in this chapter is to take the pain out of negotiating and to get the best deal for you. Of course, you could be lucky. A buyer could simply fall in love with your property and offer full price and just what you want in terms. But, quite frankly, that's not the way it usually works. In the vast majority of deals, it's now time to slug it out.

## Do You Have a Tentative Fallback Position?

In any negotiations there are winners and there are losers. Often the losers don't even know they lost for days or weeks after. But the winners always know they won. The reason is simple: The winners define winning before they start.

In your case, you must know what you want. And in the event you cannot get it, you must also create a tentative fallback position of the minimum you will accept.

### TRAP

The word *tentative* is important here. You never know what the buyers will offer. Consequently it's a mistake to form a rigid fallback position, saying, "I'll not take a penny less, no matter what!" Maybe the buyers will offer you less than you want, but in a creative scheme that you had never considered and that has all sorts of other possibilities. Be open and consider all offers.

### Are You Ready to Bargain?

Let's face up to it. The price you're asking for your home and the terms you're demanding are part realism and part hope. What you must now do is get more realistic. Let's say that houses like yours have been selling in the $60,000 to $65,000 price range. So you put your house up for $65,000. That's hope. Now an offer's coming in. You've got to understand that to be realistic, you might have to accept $60,000.

**TIP**

You never know how things are going to go and what you will do until you're in the heat of battle. I've sat with sellers who were staunchly determined not to accept a penny less than their asking price. Then, as soon as a much lower offer was made, they fawned all over the buyer's broker in their eagerness to accept. Be prepared for the unexpected, even in your own reactions.

## Can You Handle the Pressure?

Assuming that the offer is going to be presented by an agent (usually both the buyer's agent and your agent—the seller's agent—are present), you should be aware of the subtle pressures that can be brought to bear on you. Remember, after all, that neither agent gets a penny unless you agree to the offer.

In most cases where I've been present when an offer is being presented, the buyer's agent begins with a statement something like this: "I'm sure you'll agree with me that this is an excellent offer, probably the best offer that you can expect to get at this time. When you've had a chance to look it over thoroughly, I'm sure you'll realize how generous the buyer has been."

You could be asking $200,000 and the buyer could be offering $100,000. You could be asking all cash and the buyer could be demanding that you carry 100 percent financing. Still, when the deal is presented, it always seems to be a "good" offer, the "best" offer, the most "favorable and generous" offer, and so on.

I once knew a very good agent who, when faced with presenting an offer that was far off the mark, would always begin by asking the sellers, "Are you creative people?" Most of us are hard-pressed to answer that we're not creative. When the sellers replied "yes," the agent would continue. "I knew it. I knew you'd be willing to look at this offer with an open mind, because it's a creative offer."

The number of different ways to present an offer are unlimited, but it all usually comes down to the same thing. The agent tries to get you into a good mood, a mood of acceptance, and then hits you with the troubles.

## How Do I Receive an Offer?

Most sellers have no idea how to receive an offer—called a sales agreement, a purchase offer, or sometimes a deposit receipt. In most cases, they sit there dumbly while the agent puts a copy filled with clauses and tiny writing in front of them and then proceeds to read through it line by line, often obscuring some of the most salient points.

The correct way to receive an offer is to take charge and direct the proceedings. Once in charge, you can quickly find out what the strong and weak points of the offer are and then start making your decisions.

When the agent begins, "This is how I like to proceed..." interject with the following or similar comment: "This is my house and I want to proceed in the following manner." Then list what you want to know in the order of importance to you. Here's a handy list of information items prioritized in the order you may wish to receive them.

### Order for Receiving Information
### About the Offer

1. Deposit: How much and who has it? (Is it a serious offer, as evidenced by a sufficient deposit?)

2. Price: What exactly are the buyers offering?

3. Down payment: Cash, and if not, why not?

4. Terms: New first loan? Any seller financing?

5. Occupancy: How soon do I have to get out?

6. Contingencies: Is there anything that could weaken the deal?

As you go through the above questions, be sure you understand the answers given to you. When you don't understand something, ask for an explanation. If you still don't understand, don't be hesitant to ask to have it explained again and again. Only a fool is afraid to ask a question when his or her money is at stake.

### TIP

Don't act hastily. You may hear a price substantially lower than what you're asking. The tendency is to throw up your hands and say, "No, never!"

That's a mistake. Even if the price is low, the terms may make up for it, or vice versa. You almost never want to turn down an offer cold. Always try to counter.

## How Do I Tell a Good Offer from a Bad One?

If you've already prepared yourself with a tentative fallback position, you'll know pretty fast whether the offer being presented is immediately acceptable to you or whether you're going to have to probe to see if it has some fine points in your favor not initially brought out.

Usually, however, offers aren't great or terrible. They're somewhere in between, with good points and bad points. All of which means it's not usually an easy call to decide if the offer should be accepted or not.

The buyers may give you some things you want in exchange for demanding others that you don't want to give up. For example, the buyers may give you your price, but insist on onerous terms such as a long-term mortgage carried back by you at a low interest rate. You have to decide. Is it worth accepting such terms in order to get price?

Or the buyers may insist that you be out of the house within 30 days. But, you protest, the kids are in school. You need at least 90 days. The agent makes it quite clear that the buyers have to be in within 30 days because they're moving into the area in that time. The agent says they won't compromise. (Everyone will compromise a little.) Do you want to sell enough to move twice—once to a rental and a second time to your next home?

These are just a few of the trade-offs you may encounter. To help you make a decision, try the following decision-making procedure.

### Seller's Decision Maker

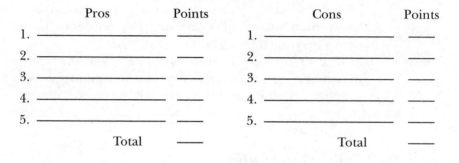

| Pros | Points | | Cons | Points |
|------|--------|---|------|--------|
| 1. ——————— —— | | | 1. ——————— —— | |
| 2. ——————— —— | | | 2. ——————— —— | |
| 3. ——————— —— | | | 3. ——————— —— | |
| 4. ——————— —— | | | 4. ——————— —— | |
| 5. ——————— —— | | | 5. ——————— —— | |
| Total —— | | | Total —— | |

List the pros and cons of the offer on this or a similar sheet. Of course, the assigning of points to issues is going to be arbitrary and you may feel that it's silly to do it. If so, then at least consider listing the pros and cons so you can see what the trade-offs are. The use of points is just an attempt to quantify the issues so that you can see at a glance which are more important and whether the preponderance of points is for or against.

## How Do I Handle Contingency Clauses?

In an offer, a contingency clause (also sometimes called a "subject to" clause) is usually a bad phrase if you're a seller. A contingency clause means just what it says—the offer is contingent on some act happening which is described in the clause.

A contingency clause is normally handwritten into the offer and is an additional condition (additional to all the boilerplate that's already part of the document). Sometimes it's written on the back of the document and initialed by the buyers. Be very careful of contingency clauses.

**TRAP**

Contingency clauses are often misunderstood by sellers because they are written in instead of being part of the prepared form of the offer. Be sure you understand all the implications of a contingency clause before you accept or reject it. If necessary, hold off making a decision on the offer until you've had your lawyer look at it and explain it to you.

## What Are Some Typical Contingencies?

- The buyers will purchase contingent on selling (translate: as soon as they sell) their present home. This is a very weak offer, because it means the sale of your house depends on the sale of another house with another set of sellers and buyers.

- The buyers will purchase contingent on their getting new financing—if they're already qualified, perhaps an excellent offer.

- The buyers will purchase contingent on Uncle Tod's cow delivering a new calf—a frivolous offer.

Contingency clauses are ways for the buyers (and sometimes the sellers) to get out of the deal. When buyers insist on a contingency clause it's like telling you, "Yes we'll buy, maybe." It's the maybe that's the killer.

Your goal is to get as few of the buyers' contingency clauses as possible into the agreement and to limit by time and performance those which are included. Let's look at that more closely.

## Limiting the Contingency Clauses

Smart buyers will put few contingency clauses into an agreement—foolish or nervous buyers put many. If you have many (more than two) in your offer to purchase, then you need to be particularly wary.

How do you handle contingency clauses? My suggestion is that you examine each one carefully and ask yourself three questions:

1.  Is the contingency reasonable? Making the purchase contingent upon getting financing is reasonable. Making it subject to Uncle Tod coming down and looking at the house in the next month or two isn't.

2.  Does this contingency negate the value of the offer? The buyers offer all cash, contingent upon their final approval of the property sometime before closing. There's no deal here, since the buyers can refuse the property at their option at any time.

3.  Can I live with the contingency or should I limit it? You can limit the contingency by insisting that it be performed within a specified time, say 7 days.

**TIP**

Remember, the offer to purchase is just that—an offer. You're not compelled to accept. The offer has no binding effect on you until you sign.

**TRAP**

Once you change the offer in any way, even something so simple as to put a time limit on a contingency, you have effectively declined the offer. What you write in is now a counteroffer, which must be submitted to the buyers and which they are under no obligation to accept.

If for any reason you can't live with the contingency as it now stands (it's not reasonable, or it negates the rest of the offer), then you must take action. The action that you may want to take is to turn down the offer and make a counteroffer.

## How Do I Make a Counteroffer?

When an offer to purchase is presented to you, you really have only three choices:

1. You can accept it exactly as it is.
2. You can reject it.
3. You can reject it and then counter with an offer of your own.

Notice that *you cannot accept it and make changes in it.* As soon as you make any changes at all to the offer presented by the buyers, it's a brand new offer. You may, for example, like the offer—only the buyers want you out by the 20th, which is a Friday; so you change it to the 21st, which is a Saturday, to give yourself more time to move. You've created a counteroffer.

When you reject the buyers' offer, they have every right to simply walk away from the potential deal. They wanted the date to be Friday the 20th so *they* would have time to move. They won't budge. Besides, in the interim they've found a house they like more than yours, so they're not interested anymore. You've lost the deal.

**TIP**

If you possibly can live with it, it's usually a good idea to accept the offer as it is presented. This assumes, of course, that the price, terms, and contingencies are all within your parameters. In other words, if the deal is very close to what you want, you may be making a mistake by trying to get the last penny or the last favorable term. By going for everything you want with a counteroffer, you risk losing what otherwise may be a sure deal.

A counter is a separate new offer. Only this time, instead of the buyers making an offer to you, you are making an offer to them.

This is somewhat confusing, since many agents write the counteroffer right on the back of the original offer, adding language to the effect that "seller accepts offer with the following changes." Then the changes are listed. The trouble is that it all sounds like you've accepted something.

In truth, you've rejected the offer and are presenting a new offer to the buyer. However, psychologically, many agents feel that if the new offer comes back on the same document and it appears that there are only a few changes, the buyers might be more willing to accept it. This is probably good psychology, although it makes for messy offers, particularly if the buyers then recounter your offer.

The important thing to remember is that each time you counter and each time the buyers counter, it's a new offer, regardless of how similar to the old offers it may be. You may end up only $100 apart. But, if one of you disagrees, there is no deal.

## When Should I Counter?

There's only one time to counter and that's when you can't accept the offer that's presented. In my opinion, you should almost never reject an offer flat out without a counter. To simply say no doesn't give the buyers an opening to come back. Maybe the first lowball offer was tentative on their part. They were just seeing if you were desperate enough to sell at a ridiculously low price. Now they're ready to come back with a higher offer. But, if you don't counter, they may feel you're unwilling to budge at all, that you're unreasonable and impossible to deal with. They may go elsewhere.

**TIP**

In a very hot market, some savvy sellers do reject offers for less than full price. They're assuming that given the market, they should be able to get exactly what they are asking and the only way to convince a buyer of this is to give a flat-out rejection. I've seen this work, although you'd better be sure of your market before you try it.

A few years ago I was selling a small home in San Jose, California. It was a rental property and I hadn't really seen it in a few years, although I did stop by just prior to putting it on the market to judge the condition and set a price that I thought was fairly reasonable. I listed it with a local broker for a price of $115,000.

Almost 2 months later the broker called to say that he had an offer. When I got together with the agents, a seller's broker and a buyer's broker, I discovered that while the terms were acceptable, the offer was for $97,000, considerably less than I thought the property was worth.

The buyer's agent pointed out that this and that was wrong with the property, that it had been a rental and had been beaten up, and that $97,000 was all that it was worth. My seller's agent sat quietly and never commented. When I asked for his advice, he said, "Better take it. It's the first offer in nearly 2 months."

Both agents advocated the offer. However, having examined the market and the house, I considered the offer frivolous. While the property might not bring the full $115,000 I was asking, it surely should bring something close.

I was tempted to simply reject the offer out of hand, since the offering price and my asking price were so far apart that I was almost insulted. However, I concealed my feelings and instead counteroffered. I countered at $114,000, $1000 less than my asking price.

My reasoning was that the offer might be frivolous, someone trying to steal the property for nothing. If that were the case, I would never hear from the buyers again. Alternatively, it might be a serious offer from a buyer who wanted to know how desperate I was to sell.

To my amazement, the buyer recountered at $113,000, up $16,000 from the previous offer and within $2000 of my original asking price! I accepted.

The moral here is that you as a seller never know what buyers are thinking and unless you give buyers the benefit of the doubt with a counteroffer, you could be passing up an otherwise good deal.

## What Should I Counter On?

There are usually four areas in which you may want to make a counteroffer:

Price

Terms

Occupancy

Contingencies

Remember, however, that if you make a counter in even just one of these areas, you've rejected the buyers' offer in all the rest and they may decide, on second thought, that they want to change some of the other areas or simply walk away.

## Countering on Price

Price is usually the number-one concern for both buyers and sellers. Yes, you want and should get your price. Just remember, however, that the buyers feel the same way.

### TRAP

Beware of a little game that sometimes occurs with offers. It's called "split the difference." In this game someone offers you less than you're asking. For example, you're asking $100,000 and they offer you $90,000. Since you had thought to get only $95,000 out of the deal anyhow, you decide to split the difference and counter at $95,000.

Now, however, the buyers decide to split the difference again and they counter at $92,500. What are you going to do? If you split the difference again, you're going to counter at $93,750, less than you want. If you reject the offer flat out, you may lose the deal. Splitting the difference has done you in.

It's important never to reveal your rock-bottom price. If the buyers offer less than you're asking, perhaps you may want to counter at a price lower than you were originally asking, but still higher than your rock-bottom price so that you can have some maneuvering room.

## Countering on Terms

Terms might offer the greatest flexibility. Most often the buyers are seeking a new loan and plan to pay cash down to the loan. But many times they are asking you to carry part of the financing, perhaps a second or third mortgage for a portion of the down payment.

Just remember that everything is negotiable here. If you're willing to carry back some of the financing, you may agree to their proposed terms, but change the length of the loan or the interest rate. (The shorter the mortgage and the higher the interest rate, generally speaking, the better the deal for you.)

## TIP

If you carry back "paper" (a second or lesser mortgage), try to see that it includes a monthly payment at least equal to the interest owed and that it also includes a *late penalty* for failure to make the payment on time. This will often make the mortgage more salable should you decide at a later date to cash it in.

### Counter on Occupancy

Although it seems a simple thing, I've seen many deals fall apart because of a disagreement over occupancy. You need to stay, the sellers need to get in, and neither will budge—the deal goes south.

If you want to sell your home, you have to be prepared to be flexible in terms of the timing. You have to be willing to give up on your schedule, if it means making the deal.

I've seen sellers move out early and live in a motel or rented house in order to make a deal. I've seen sellers stay 6 months longer than they planned (and pay rent to the buyers) because the buyers couldn't get in right away. I've even seen sellers give the buyers a bonus if they would agree to wait a few months extra before moving in.

There is really no reason an occupancy problem should ruin a deal, as long as you're flexible. Here are some alternatives:

1. Change your own time plans.
2. Move and rent for a while.
3. Stay and rent from the buyers.
4. Pay the buyers a bonus to change their plans.
5. Rent a motel suite for the buyers until you can move out.

Think of it this way: Is it worth a little inconvenience to sell your house?

### Countering on the Contingencies

In the counteroffer there are two ways to handle an unwanted contingency clause: the straightforward approach and the diplomatic approach.

You can be straightforward and simply cross out the contingency. You won't accept it. This states your position clearly, but it may offend the buyer and cost you a deal.

### TIP

A very successful builder friend had an absolute rule regarding contingencies: He refused to sign any agreement with a contingency in it, no matter how innocuous the clause was. He said it was just a way out for the buyer. It's something to remember.

On the other hand, you can be diplomatic and attempt to limit the contingency. The buyers have inserted a contingency which says that the purchase is subject to a great aunt coming down and approving the bedroom she'll be living in when the house is purchased. Fine. You have no problem with that. Accept the contingency, only add that the great aunt has to give her approval within 3 days.

You haven't insulted the buyers. You haven't suggested that the contingency was a ploy to allow them to get out of the deal. You've gone along with it. You've agreed to take your house off the market for 3 days while the buyers satisfy the great aunt or whomever.

But you've also made it clear that you mean business and that you don't have time for frivolous antics. After 3 days they either remove the contingency or they lose the house.

### TIP

Time is the great limiter of contingencies.

Or the buyers say they want a structural engineer to examine your home to be sure that the last earthquake (you live in California) hasn't damaged it. Instead of simply saying no, you won't do that (which only makes the buyers suspicious), agree—provided that they pay the engineer and that they approve the inspection within a week.

Now you've limited the contingency by action and time.

Limiting the contingencies makes it appear that you're going along with the buyers' wishes, all the while making the offer more acceptable to you.

### Specifying How a Contingency Is to Be Removed

If you're limiting a contingency by time, be sure that you specify how that contingency is to be removed. For example, the sellers want a soil inspection to check for drainage and flooding. You agree, but specify that they must provide you with written approval of a completed report within, for example, a week. Otherwise, the deal is off.

**TIP**

Contingencies work both ways. There may come a time when you want to add a contingency to your benefit. For example, the buyers want you to supply a termite clearance, which is pretty standard and usually a necessary part of getting a new loan. But you're afraid that there might be extensive termite damage. You don't mind spending a few hundreds bucks to clean up the termites, but you might balk at spending a few thousand. You might write in a contingency that limits your costs in supplying the clearance to, say, $1000. If it's more than that amount, the deal's off. (Be careful that when you signed your listing agreement you didn't already agree to a termite clearance regardless of the costs.)

## What Do I Do If the Buyers Simply Walk Away from the Deal?

What do you do when you've been too clever? The buyers made an offer and you countered at lower than your asking price, but higher than your rock-bottom price (hoping to pump a few more bucks out of the deal). You fully expected the buyers either to accept or to counter back. But instead, the buyers have done nothing! Apparently they are simply rejecting your offer and looking elsewhere. Does that mean the deal is dead?

Not necessarily. There is nothing to keep you from making a second counteroffer even though the buyers have rejected the first and have not countered back.

Of course, it puts you in a rather silly and weak position. You counter $66,000, for example, and when the buyers flat out refuse, you counter $64,000. It's bound to make the buyers wonder just how low you'll go if they just hang tight. Maybe your next counter will be for $60,000!

**TIP**

When you are making desperation counters, I believe a good rule of thumb is to make only *one*. Tell the buyers (through the agent, if possible) that you really want to sell and that you hoped that they would counter. However, since they didn't, you're going to make them one last, final offer—your very best deal, so to speak. Make it perfectly clear that this is your fallback position offer. If they don't take it, there won't be any others forthcoming. Sometimes it works. Of course, it raises this question: What if the buyers now counter at a lower price or terms? (Selling real estate can be so aggravating!)

Ultimately, as always, you have to decide on the minimum for which you'll sell your property. You can't go any lower than you can go.

## What Happens When I Accept the Offer?

You don't accept an offer until both parties sign the exact same sales agreement. For you, until the pen touches the paper, and actually for a short time afterward, there is no deal.

Until you sign, you can refuse to accept the offer. (However, if the offer is for the price and terms you listed the property for, you could still be liable for a commission to the agent!)

It's important to understand, however, that the deal isn't made exactly when you sign. Rather, it's made when the agent (or you) communicates the fact that you've signed to the buyers. In practice, this means that usually the agent immediately calls the buyers to tell them you've accepted and then takes them a signed (by you) copy of the sales agreement. Technically speaking, the buyers can withdraw the offer anytime before they learn of your acceptance (just as you can withdraw a counteroffer anytime before the buyers accept it).

Sometimes the buyers (or you) are a long distance away. To facilitate the deal, the negotiations may be carried out over the phone. I've agreed to deals from thousands of miles away and then sent a copy of the signed agreement by either express mail or fax machine. Distances shouldn't keep a deal from happening.

## Keep a Copy

The agent (or the buyers) must give you a copy of everything you sign. Be sure that you get that copy and that you hang onto it. Later on, if there should be some dispute over what was actually agreed upon (particularly if counteroffers were scrawled over the original offer), your copy will be your protection. Get it and make sure it contains the signatures of the buyers over the last and final counteroffer.

## Moving On

Once you've gotten a signed sales agreement, you're halfway home (but not all the way). Now you have to open escrow, deliver clear title, make sure the buyers get their financing, and do those hundred other small things that are necessary before the deal closes.

No, you can't say you've sold your house until the title is recorded and you've gotten your check, but at this stage, you can kick back and relax a bit. Hopefully, the hardest part is over.

For more information on negotiating, try my book *Tips and Traps When Negotiating Real Estate* (McGraw-Hill, 1995).

# 10

# Perils of
# Seller Financing

Just a few years ago if someone had asked me about seller financing, I would have suggested that it was an excellent way to facilitate a sale and to get a high-interest-paying note as well. Today, I'm not so sure. I've seen so many seller-financed deals go sour that I'm beginning to think that it's something to avoid, if at all possible. Here's why.

## What Is Seller Financing?

When you go into the grocery store and buy a jar of mayonnaise, normally you would pay all cash. You'd give the clerk your $1.50 or $2.00 or whatever, take the mayonnaise, and that would be the end of the transaction.

Selling real estate is rarely that simple, particularly in today's high-priced market. Few, very few buyers, have cash to pay for the purchase of your home. Rather, they plan to finance most of the purchase price (typically 80 to 90 percent of it).

The usual route for financing is to go to an institutional lender—a bank, a savings and loan, or a mortgage banker. This lender gives the buyer the money in exchange for a trust deed (a variation of a mortgage, but more commonly used) on the property. The buyer now gives you the money (which you use to pay off your existing mortgage and costs of sale, keeping what remains for yourself) and the deal is made.

However, sometimes the buyers won't or can't go to the institutional lender. Instead, they come to you and say, "Seller, please finance my purchase of your home." As explained in an earlier chapter, they may want you to carry back a second or third mortgage for a portion of the purchase price. If you own your home free and clear, they may even want you to carry back a first mortgage.

Seller financing is when you receive "paper" (mortgage or trust deed) instead of cash for your sale. Of course, the real question for you, the seller, is: Should I do it? Should I finance my property for the buyer?

## The Buyers' Motivation

The first thing you should look at when you're considering carrying back "paper" is the reason that buyers have for asking you to do so. Typically the reasons are all bad, for you. Here are a few:

### Reasons Buyers Want You to Carry the Financing

1. The buyers have bad credit and can't get an institutional loan.
2. The buyers can't qualify (don't have enough income) to get an institutional loan for enough money to make the sale.
3. The buyers don't have enough cash for the down payment.
4. Interest rates are so high that the buyers can't qualify for a mortgage.
5. The buyers are investors and they are looking to get a better deal by having you carry the financing.

## Your Motivation

Notice that in every case the reason for your carrying paper is to the buyers' advantage. You do it, in other words, not to help yourself, but to help the buyers. Why then, should you bother?

### Reasons for a Seller to Carry Financing

1. You can make a deal that otherwise couldn't be made.
2. You can often get a high-interest-paying loan in your favor.

Let's look at the sellers' reasons for carrying financing more closely.

## Carrying Financing to Make a Deal

My friend Ann has a house in the Dallas, Texas, area. As of this writing this area of the country has been recovering economically, but just a few years ago it was a catastrophe. Falling oil prices caused the housing market to collapse. Very quickly a buyer's market emerged.

Ann, seeing what was happening, tried to get out ahead of the crowd. She put her house on the market as soon as prices started to waver. Even so, there were few buyers.

Ann saw that things were only getting worse and she realized that time was against her, so she told her agent that she was willing to carry all the down payment in the form of paper. A buyer only had to pay closing costs to move in. Here is how the deal played out:

| What Ann paid in cash | | What Ann received | |
|---|---|---|---|
| Her closing costs | $ 4,000 | Second mortgage | $35,000 |
| Commission | 6,000 | (her equity) | |
| Total cash | $10,000 | | |

Notice that it cost Ann $10,000 in cash out of pocket to make the sale. However, since she was getting a second mortgage for $35,000, she felt that she was coming out ahead. (The second paid 11 percent interest, which was far more than she could have gotten at the bank at the time.)

The economy continued to deteriorate in the area, however, and within 6 months the buyers lost their jobs. They decided to move to California. They put the house up for resale.

However, they quickly saw that the housing market had gotten so bad that there was little chance to sell soon, if at all. So they simply packed up and left.

The first Ann heard of this was when she didn't receive her monthly second mortgage payment. She waited a week, thinking it had been lost in the mail, then she called the buyers of her house. Their phone was disconnected.

She mailed a letter to the buyers asking for an explanation. The letter was returned—there was no forwarding address. She called the agent who had handled the sale and asked him to investigate. He reported back that the house was locked up and empty. And it looked like quite a mess inside. He then gave Ann two rather bleak options:

1. She could begin foreclosure proceedings (a fairly swift process in Texas) and take back the property. However, to do so she would have to make up the back payments on the first mortgage (several thousand dollars at that point—the buyers hadn't been paying on the first) and pay foreclosure costs, another thousand or so. Once she got the house back in her name, it would probably cost her another $3000 to fix it up and put it into good enough shape to make another attempt at reselling.

2. She could simply walk away from the property as the buyers had done and *lose all of her $35,000 second mortgage.*

Ann immediately ruled out option number 2. She wasn't going to lose $35,000. She caught a flight to Texas and met with the agent. He showed her the house; it would need repainting and recarpeting throughout—probably at a cost closer to $5000 than to $3000. Then the agent pointed out that the market had gone completely cold. Nothing was selling—everything was in foreclosure. If Ann paid the $10,000 or so it would cost to get the property back and fix it up, she might not be able to sell it for a year or two, if then.

"I'll rent it," was her reply. The agent shook his head sadly. Everyone was trying to rent. Landlords were offering 2 and 3 months' free rent just to get people to move in.

In the end, Ann realized the futility of it all. She gave up, lost her $35,000, and wrote it off to her education in real estate—a very expensive lesson.

The point of Ann's story is that in today's marketplace, if you finance a house in order to make a deal, sometimes you end up with a deal that would have better been not made. In the end you could lose everything.

The reason goes back to the motivations of buyers. Top-notch buyers, those who have credit and cash, often don't want seller financing. They want to put down the cash to keep their payments low and they don't have any problem qualifying for a mortgage.

On the other hand, problem buyers who don't have cash or who can't get new financing are looking for seller financing. Thus, very often sellers who carry back paper are in reality getting problem buyers, people who can't (or won't) keep up the property or make the payments. These may be people who already have such bad credit that they don't mind walking away if things get rough.

### TRAP

There's a whole different category of buyers—investors. A spate of "get rich quick in real estate" seminars and books has spawned a group of so-called investors whose whole attitude seems to be "I can get rich in real estate by taking advantage of sellers." These people often buy property with seller financing, then refinance the property under the seller's loan (we'll see how shortly), take the cash and leave. The poor seller is stuck in a position even worse than Ann's, for now the property has financing on it, frequently for far more than it's worth!

## Carrying Financing for Investment

This is not to say that all seller financing is bad. Sometimes, depending on your motivation for using it, it can turn out quite well.

For example, I have another friend, Chuck, who was about to retire. He had social security, but wasn't sure that would be enough to live on during retirement. He wanted another source of income. His biggest asset was the equity in his home, which was all paid off. Chuck's goal was to sell his home, put the money he received in the bank, and live off the interest.

However, at the time the banks' highest interest rate was 8 percent. Since Chuck had about $125,000 that he would get from the sale of the home, that meant he would receive roughly $10,000 a year. He had hoped for more.

When it came time to sell, however, the agent suggested that instead of looking for a buyer who would get a new institutional loan, Chuck should carry the first mortgage. Firsts were then paying about 11 percent interest, which would translate to about $14,000 a year in income for him. In addition, if he made the loan for 20 or even 30 years, he could be fairly assured of a steady income for a long time to come. Chuck was in the Northern California market, which was warm at the time, and the agent felt a sale wouldn't be too hard to make, with or without seller financing.

Chuck thought it was a good idea.

When buyers were found, the agent qualified them just as if they were getting a new institutional loan. They had to have good credit, they had to have sufficient income to "qualify" (roughly three times the monthly payment after all long-term debt, such as car payments), and they had to have the normal down payment.

The buyers purchased and Chuck carried back the financing. It's been nearly 6 years now and Chuck's monthly check hasn't been late once.

## Two Different Outcomes

A large part of the reason behind Chuck's success and Ann's failure has to do with their motivation in carrying back paper. In Ann's case, she felt it was the only way to make a sale. Consequently, she was willing to accept less than desirable buyers.

In Chuck's case, however, the motivation was long-term income. Chuck was willing to sell only to buyers who were totally qualified. Of course, it must be pointed out that Chuck was selling in a warm market while Ann's market was cold. This, however, only highlights the problem with much seller financing—it is done out of desperation.

**TIP**

Be aware of your motives when you carry back paper. If you're desperate to sell and use seller financing to attract a buyer, be aware you might get a less than desirable buyer. You might end up losing more than you gain by making the sale.

## How to Use Seller Financing to Your Advantage

Thus far we've looked at two examples of what can go wrong and what can go right with seller financing. There are, however, a whole host of variables in between. We'll consider some of these now. (At the end of the chapter is a list of items to consider before you offer to finance your buyer.)

### 1. The Seller Who Outsmarts the Bad Buyer

I know of several sellers who purposely look for unqualified buyers. Their goal is to sell their property to a buyer in the hopes that the buyer will default after a year or more so that they can get the property back through foreclosure. In this way, they can keep reselling the same property over and over!

There are two catches to making this plan work. First, the sellers have to keep their costs down. These sellers typically sell FSBO, on their own, so they don't have any commission to pay. Their only expenses are the closing costs when they sell and the foreclosure costs later on if they have to take the property back.

Second, they get a large enough down payment from the buyers to cover all their costs plus a profit.

Since it's often a year or more before the buyers default and the sellers foreclose, the market price of the home hopefully goes up. That means that each time the sellers get the property back, they are able to resell for a higher price!

I'm not advocating this approach. I'm simply mentioning it to point out that if you want to play the game as a seller, you can play it to win.

### 2. The Seller Who Converts Paper into Cash

Paper can be converted to cash, depending on a number of variables. Here's how sellers can take advantage of this conversion.

The sellers have a house to sell which they feel is worth $100,000 on the market in a cash deal. However, they realize it may take a while to find a cash buyer, so they put it up for sale at $105,000 and agree that they'll take partial paper.

| Cash sale | Paper sale |
|---|---|
| $20,000 cash down | $10,000 cash down |
| | $15,000 second mortgage carried by seller |
| $80,000 new first from bank or S&L | $80,000 new first from bank or S&L |
| $100,000 | $105,000 sales price |

The buyers, presumably, are willing to pay a little more for the house, since they don't have to put up all cash down.

Once the sale is made, the seller waits at least 6 months, during which time the buyer (hopefully) makes regular monthly payments on the $15,000 second mortgage. Then the seller sells that second mortgage to a buyer of seconds for cash—in this case, $10,000 cash. The seller ends up with the same $20,000 in cash as he or she would have received in a cash sale, except that there's a 6-month delay. (However, during that 6 months the buyer pays a good rate of interest on the money.)

The advantage of this sale is that the seller, hopefully, is able to move the house faster by offering to carry back some of the paper than by waiting for an all-cash buyer.

**Why the 6-month wait?**   I'm sure some readers are wondering why the seller waited 6 months before converting the second to cash. Indeed, the seller could have converted that note to cash in escrow and this is sometimes done. However, buyers of second notes (investors who are looking to make a higher interest on their cash) are wary of "unseasoned" seconds. They don't know if the buyer will actually make the payments or will simply default. Buyers of seconds don't normally want to get involved in foreclosure. (An exception is the investor who buys seconds in properties where the owners have huge equities, hoping that those owners will default.)

If you sell a second mortgage in escrow, the buyer of that second will normally pay less than if you let it "age" for a minimum of 6 months. Our seller waited 6 months to be sure that at least $10,000 cash could be realized from the $15,000 second.

**Why only $10,000 for a $15,000 note?**   A second question many readers are sure to be asking is why didn't the buyer of the second pay the full $15,000 in cash? Why was there a $5000 discount?

The reason has to do with yield and risk. Yield is the actual percentage rate of interest that a buyer of seconds gets. It is computed in a fairly complex formula that takes into account the interest rate, the amount of cash paid out, and the term of the second. For example, a second mortgage for 3 years may have a stated interest rate of 12 percent.

However, because of the risk of foreclosure in the second-mortgage market, an investor may demand a yield of 18 percent. How does he or she get that yield from a 12 percent mortgage?

The answer is by discounting the second mortgage. A 12 percent mortgage which pays $15,000 at maturity, but which costs the buyer of that mortgage only $10,000 in cash, will in fact yield upward of 18 percent interest. (The 18 percent is figured on the $10,000 actually invested.)

It's much like zero-coupon government bonds. You pay less than the face value of the bond. The difference is computed as your interest rate over the term.

Thus by discounting the second mortgage, the seller is able to find an investor who is willing to buy it for cash.

**TIP**

 The trick with offers to carry back a second with the intention of converting it to cash is to get a high enough second. You need to have enough leeway so that when you sell at discount, you get out the cash you need.

**What makes a second mortgage salable?**   Finally, it's important to understand that simply taking back a second mortgage as part of seller financing doesn't guarantee you can resell it. Here's what investors are looking for in seconds:

1. High interest rate. The higher the better.

2. A 3- to 5-year term. Shorter terms mean that the investor has to turn his or her money around too often. Longer terms mean that the money is tied up against an uncertain future when interest rate fluctuations could reduce the value of the second.

3. A late penalty. This is important. The second should contain a money penalty if the buyers are more than a couple of weeks

late in their payment. The reason is simple. If there is no penalty, then each time the buyers are late, the holder of the second has only one option—start foreclosure, an expensive proposition. On the other hand, if the second has a penalty, it is easy to enforce and encourages prompt payment.

4. Proper documents. Improper documents or documents that are improperly executed account for more failures of seconds than people realize. If you're giving a second as part of the sale, be sure you have a competent attorney check out the documents.

### 3. The Seller Who Takes Back a Balloon Payment

Finally, there is the seller who helps out the buyer and himself as well. This seller is aware that buyers have trouble qualifying for mortgages. So the seller offers the buyers an "interest only" second mortgage. The buyers will pay, for example, for 3 years, interest only. After that time the full amount of the mortgage is due. In other words, the sellers get interest for 3 years, then all of the principle comes due! This is called a balloon payment, when one payment is much higher than the others.

The buyers at the end of the 3 years normally have to refinance to get enough cash to pay off the balloon second. Many sellers at the end of the 3 years will offer to extend the mortgage for an additional 3 years at the then current interest rate.

In this way the seller preserves capital all the while receiving a good interest rate on it.

**TRAP**

 Beware of mortgage assumptions. In our examples, seller financing consisted of giving the buyers a second mortgage as part of the down payment when they either got a new first or assumed an FHA or VA (government insured or guaranteed) mortgage. Seller financing, however, *did not involve buyers assuming existing conventional (nongovernment) first mortgages.*

The reason is simple. In today's marketplace almost no conventional loans are really assumable. When you sell your house, chances are the buyers cannot take over your existing first mortgage unless it's a VA or FHA (and then there may be restrictions). If the mortgage does provide for an "assumption," chances are the buyers have to requalify, pay new costs, and pay the then current interest rate—which is equivalent to getting a new mortgage.

## Checklist for Seller Financing

|  | YES | NO |
|---|---|---|
| 1. Are you getting the current market interest rate for seconds? | [ ] | [ ] |

Check with agents, with the local paper under ads for seconds for sale, and with mortgage brokers to find the current rate.

|  | YES | NO |
|---|---|---|
| 2. Are you giving the right term? | [ ] | [ ] |

Seconds over 5 years are sometimes considered too long term to be salable.

|  | YES | NO |
|---|---|---|
| 3. Have you checked out the buyers' credit? | [ ] | [ ] |

You can get a credit report either directly from a credit agency or through your agent. If the buyers have any bad credit at all, you're significantly increasing your risk of having to take the property back.

|  | YES | NO |
|---|---|---|
| 4. Have you gotten an estimate of foreclosure costs in your state? | [ ] | [ ] |

There are professionals who specialize in handling foreclosures. They often advertise under Real Estate in the classified section of papers. Or you can contact an escrow officer or a real estate agent who can direct you to one. Find out your likely costs now, before you commit.

|  | YES | NO |
|---|---|---|
| 5. Are the buyers putting a lot of cash into the property? | [ ] | [ ] |

The more cash the buyers put in, the more committed they will be to holding onto the property and avoiding default. Beware of buyers who put no cash down.

YES      NO

6. Are you careful to *avoid* having a subordination clause
   in your second?      [ ]      [ ]

A subordination clause makes your second "subordinate" to another mortgage. What this means is that the buyers could refinance the first for more money, making your second virtually worthless. Avoid this like the plague.

YES      NO

7. Are your documents correct?      [ ]      [ ]

The only way to have any sense of security here is to have your documents examined by (if not prepared by) a competent real estate attorney.

YES      NO

8. Have you consulted an attorney and a tax planner/
   accountant to inform you of the tax consequences of
   getting a second mortgage?      [ ]      [ ]

In some cases even though you got back paper, the government may treat the sale as cash and could require you to pay tax on the money that you didn't receive!

YES      NO

9. Have you consulted with an expert on seller financing
   in your area to see if you're handling the deal correctly? [ ]      [ ]

Each state has somewhat different laws and rules regarding second mortgages. Be sure you're in compliance in your state.

# 11

# The Lease Option Option

Whenever the market gets tight and sellers are having trouble finding buyers, you see a lot of ads for "lease options." Sometimes they can work very well for sellers, in the near term getting a higher than market rent and in the longer term providing a buyer. On the other hand, they don't always work out as planned. We'll look at their pros and cons in this chapter.

## What Is a Lease Option?

A lease option is a combination of a rental lease on your property plus an option to buy all rolled into one neat package. (There are ready-made lease option forms available in stationery stores. However, I suggest you get an attorney to draw one up for your specific situation.) A lease states a term of rental (usually for 1 year or longer), a set amount payable monthly for the whole term, and rental conditions. An option states that at the *tenant's* option, he or she can purchase the property up to a certain date (typically 2 or 3 years in the future), typically for a price agreed upon now. Usually there is cash put up to pay for the option privilege; however, in a lease option the lease itself is often considered enough.

Typically under a lease option the tenant pays a little more than market rent each month, a portion of which is applied toward a future down payment should the tenant exercise the option portion and buy the property.

The lease option has many attractive elements for both the seller of a home and a potential buyer.

## Why Would the Buyer
## Want a Lease Option?

As noted many times earlier in this book, buyers in the United States are typically short on cash. They don't have the funds necessary to make the down payment. With a lease option, however, they can tie up a house, move in, and accumulate at least part of the down payment right along with their rent. (Remember, a portion of the rent typically goes toward the down.) Let's take an example.

### Lease Option Example

Peter and Sally want to buy your home and are agreeable to paying the $150,000 you're asking. But they don't have the necessary 10 percent down payment ($15,000). So you offer them a lease option. You'll rent it to them for $1500 a month (the lease). Of that $1500, $1000 will actually be rent and $500 will go toward a future down payment. When they have accumulated enough money for the down (after 2½ years), you will credit them with the money and they will exercise their option and buy the property.

| | |
|---|---|
| Monthly payment | $ 1500 |
|    Toward rent | $ 1000 |
|    Toward down | $ 500 |
| 30 months at $500 per month | $15,000 |

It's a neat scheme and many times it goes off without a hitch. The tenants pay the rent, accumulate the down, and are able to buy the property. It takes the buyers a little longer, but they do live in the property and, eventually, end up owning it.

## Why Would I Want to Give
## a Lease Option?

There may be more reasons than you think.

1. You have the chance for a sale in a market where sales may be hard to find. There are a lot more people out there who can pay a higher rent than can come up with a cash down. Find one of those,

agree to a lease option, and look forward to selling your house, albeit a few years down the road.

2. You immediately remove the problem of making payments on your current mortgage, taxes, and insurance. By renting out the property you get immediate income. And because the rental is for more than the rental market rate (the money that is accumulating toward the down payment), you usually have enough to make ends meet. If you've moved out of your home and are worrying about making the mortgage payments, this can be a wonderful solution.

3. You don't have to worry about maintaining the property. Remember, your tenants are the future owners. They have a vested interest in keeping it in great shape. Further, many lease option agreements provide that the tenants will pay for all minor repairs themselves.

**TIP**

You not only get the world's best tenant, but also a tenant who pays for repairs! It's a landlord's dream come true.

4. The tenants may not choose to exercise the option. After several years, for reasons we shall explore in a moment, they may decide not to buy. In that case you, the seller, get the property back, frequently in excellent shape, and get to keep all the extra money the tenants were paying in rent!

Is it any wonder that many sellers look eagerly toward a lease option as a wonderful out in a tight market?

## Are There Any Problems with the Lease Option?

Be aware that lease options are not panaceas.

### TIP

A good rule to follow in real estate as well as in life is that if something appears to be too good to be true, it usually is. That's frequently the case with a lease option.

Typically when you first enter into a lease option, things are wonderful. The tenants pay on time and are quite content. However, as time goes by, the tenants may begin to see the additional rent as a burden. It may be difficult for them to make the hefty monthly payments.

Further, unless the tenants have excellent credit, they may begin to realize that even if they accumulate enough for a down payment, they may not be able to qualify for a new mortgage, meaning they won't be able to exercise their option. (Which means they'll lose all the extra rent money they are paying.)

Once the tenants realize that there is no light at the end of the tunnel, that the purchase of your home isn't realistic, they may bail out. They may simply walk away. In so doing, they could leave your property a mess.

### TRAP

My own experience with lease options has been less than satisfactory. I've had tenants who I had qualified for financing get into financial trouble and leave, almost wrecking the home. Don't think it can't happen to you. No matter how careful you are, it's a real possibility.

Here is a list of some of the things that can go wrong with a lease option.

### Things That Can Go Wrong

1. Tenants can't make the rental payment.
2. Tenants discover, after living in the property, that they don't like it and don't want to buy it.

3. Tenants aren't qualified to get a new mortgage.

4. Mortgage rates rise and previously qualified tenants now can't get a loan.

5. Tenants stop making payments and move out, leaving property a mess.

## Can I Protect Myself?

You can do some things that will help ensure a better ending to your lease option.

### Qualify Your Tenant/Buyers

Before going through with a lease option, have your tenant/buyers visit a mortgage broker or bank and get a letter stating that they currently qualify for a mortgage big enough to make the sale. That doesn't guarantee they'll qualify later on when they try to exercise the option (rates could change, as could their financial situation), but it at least shows they have the potential of qualifying.

### Make the Rent High Enough So Tenants Can Realistically Accumulate the Down

This an important point. Say your house is selling for $200,000 and the tenant/buyers need $20,000. If the amount accumulating from extra rent is only $100 a month and the lease option runs for 3 years, they will have accumulated only $3600 by the time they need to exercise the option—not nearly enough. (And they probably won't have saved the balance on the side by themselves either.)

### TRAP

Setting the amount of the rent that goes to the future down payment too low is a recipe for failure with a lease option.

## Be Receptive to Reasonable
## Complaints About the Property

While the tenant/buyers can be expected to handle minor problems, major ones need cooperative efforts. They can handle a
leaky faucet, but what about a new roof that's needed and costs
$10,000? You'll have to work out a compromise and pay part or
most of it yourself. If you insist on the them paying for unreasonable expenses, they'll walk.

## Set a Price Now

It's not necessary to fix a price. You can agree that the price will be
what an appraiser (or the average of three real estate agents) says
it is at a future date. But that tends to make would-be tenant/buy-
ers nervous. It should do the same for you if prices have been
falling in your area.

It's important that the would-be buyers and you know what the
goal is. Maybe it's $150,000 price or $300,000 or $75,000. Both you
and the tenant/buyers need to know.

### TIP

It is possible to include an inflation clause in a price.
It's $100,000, for example, plus the cost of inflation
annually, or the increase in housing prices annually,
or whatever. Be aware, however. The prospective ten-
ant/buyers are not likely to look favorably on such a
clause.

# How Do I Handle the
# Broker's Commission?

Often people who do lease options already have their property
listed. How do you get the agent to withdraw the listing?

You could always wait until it expires. But usually the agent is
more than willing to handle the lease option for you. Indeed, the
agent may bring it to you.

Typically the agent receives a fee for the option. It's less than a sales commission, but is usually quite substantial, perhaps 1 or 2 months' rent. Further, if the buyers later exercise their option, then the agent gets the full commission. (That's why agents like this!)

## Should I Give a Lease Option?

It really depends on your goals and the market. I've known sellers who see a lease option as a way of milking money out of property they never intended to sell. They purposely get tenant/buyers who could never qualify for a loan, and get the extra rent money from them. Then, when the tenants can't exercise their option and move out, the sellers do it all over again with someone else. I'm not condoning such unscrupulous action, just pointing out that it is done.

For most of us, the lease option is a possible answer in a tight market. Just remember, however, that it's not without its problems and it's not a cureall.

# 12
# The Rental Conversion Option

You can't sell, and times are so tough you can't even find a potential buyer who will agree to a lease option on the property (or who can qualify for one). The trouble is you have to move (you've gotten a job change). What do you do?

Rent it out.

Or you're looking for an investment property and realize your present house is too small, too big, or not close enough to work. What do you do?

Convert it to a rental.

When you currently own a home, converting it to a rental may be a desperation move, but it could also prove to be a very profitable decision, as we'll see in this chapter.

## How It's Done

My friend Arlie, who owns a house in a suburb of Los Angeles, was recently transferred to Denver. He put his LA house up for sale. But the market at the time was cool and there were no takers. So what did Arlie do?

He didn't give up his new job opportunity. He didn't lose the equity in his house by letting it go to foreclosure. He rented it with the understanding that when the market improved in the LA area, he would sell it.

As it turned out, while he rented the property, Arlie was able to use it as a write-off on his taxes (there are restrictions here, so see your accountant). Later, when he eventually sold, he was able to

**131**

get a higher price than he originally had the house listed for. In effect, not selling but renting turned out to be a boon for him.

This is not to say that becoming a landlord is all peaches and cream. It can be hard work, particularly if you are forced to move some distance away. But it can be manageable. People do it all the time. I've done it many times myself. And it may be your best alternative to selling.

## But What If I Need the Money from a Sale to Buy My Next House?

You can get some of your money out, even if you rent your current home. You can get it out by refinancing.

For example, let's say that your house is worth $200,000 and you owe $100,000. Your expenses of selling might run $15,000 (including commission), so you stand to get $85,000 clear, if you could sell. You plan to use that $85,000 toward the purchase of your next house.

But your house just won't sell. The market's bad, or the neighborhood isn't terrific, or the house could be in better condition. For whatever reason, it won't sell and you certainly don't want to just walk away from all that equity.

So you refinance it. As an *owner/occupant* you are entitled to refinance your home for up to 80 percent of its current value. (If you were an investor who owned a rental property, most lenders would loan you enough only to pay off your existing mortgage and closing costs. Being an owner/occupant offers many more opportunities.)

If your home is worth $200,000 you should be able to refinance up to $160,000 (80 percent). Less your existing mortgage of $100,000 and roughly $5000 in financing expenses, you could clear about $55,000.

| | |
|---|---|
| New first mortgage | $ 160,000 |
| Less existing mortgage | − 100,000 |
| Less refinancing expenses | − 5,000 |
| Net out | $ 55,000 |

By refinancing, you could net out $55,000. Now that's considerably less than the $85,000 you might hope to net out on a sale, but it's still a fair hunk of cash and you could certainly use it as a substantial down payment on a second property.

**TIP**

You may be able to refinance even more out of your property by securing a home equity loan on it for an additional amount *after* you refinance the first. Most lenders, however, are hesitant to give a home equity loan when you already owe 80 percent of the value, so you may have to search to find one who is willing.

**TIP**

Remember, whether or not you're able to get favorable refinancing depends to a large degree on whether or not you are an owner/occupant. That means that you must secure all your financing *before* you move from your property. Once you have the mortgage on your property, most lenders don't care whether you continue to occupy it or rent it out.

## Does It Make Financial Sense?

Seeing how it works doesn't mean it will make sense to refinance. Remember, you have to make payments on the mortgage. Can you rent for enough to cover your payments?

Generally speaking, in order for a rental property to make financial sense, you must be able to cover your mortgage payment plus your property taxes plus your insurance on the property from the rental. (In the trade that's called PITI—principle, interest, taxes, and insurance.) That doesn't really mean that you break even, because you still have maintenance, advertising, clean-up, and so forth. But those expenses are usually manageable, provided the property breaks even on the PITI.

Your first task, therefore, is to learn what your PITI will be. You already know your taxes and insurance costs (presumably), so all that you need to discover is what your mortgage costs will be. That's easy. Just call up some lenders. Over the phone they'll tell you exactly what your monthly payment will be, given current mortgage rates and the amount you want to borrow.

Your second task is a bit more difficult—determining how much you can get in rent for your home. There are, however, several sources for this kind of information.

### Sources for Learning Rental Rate Information

1. Contact local agents and ask them.

2. Look for rentals in your neighborhood and ask the owners what the rental rate is.

3. Check your local paper under "Houses for Rent—Unfurnished" (unless for some reason you intend leaving your furniture). Look for homes with the same number of bedrooms and baths as yours and in similar areas and see what others are charging.

4. Check with rental bureaus in your area.

You may find that you can rent your home for $700 a month or $1000 or $3000 (depending on the area and the home).

### TIP

If you're planning to rent out your property for only a short time and need to refinance, look for an adjustable-rate mortgage (ARM) with a low "teaser" rate. This rate may be 2 to 3 percentage points below the current rate. Be aware that the teaser rate is just that. Usually within 2 years or less the mortgage interest rate rises to the current market rate. But by then, hopefully, you'll be able to sell and will have benefited from the low rate in the meantime.

Now compare your monthly anticipated mortgage payments with your monthly anticipated rent. In a moment you'll see whether renting is financially feasible or not.

## Rental Income Versus PITI

| | PITI | Rental Income |
|---|---|---|
| Mortgage(s) | $_____ | |
| Taxes | $_____ | |
| Insurance | $_____ | |
| Total | $_____ | $_____ |

If rental income is higher, if both figures are the same, or if they are even just close, you have an excellent chance of financially handling the rental of your property.

If expenses are higher, then you may want to reconsider renting.

### TIP

Don't fall into the mistaken belief that you won't have any other costs beyond PITI. As noted earlier, there will always be maintenance and fix-up expenses. However, hopefully you'll be able to write off the property (see your accountant), and this will more than make up for the other expenses.

### TRAP

If it turns out that your PITI expenses are far higher than your rental income, don't decide to "damn the torpedoes, full speed ahead!" When expenses exceed rental income, you move into negative cash flow territory. That means that each month just to pay the mortgage, taxes, and insurance, you have to take money out of your own pocket. While this may seem easy to do when looking at it theoretically, it's quite different when you're faced with actually spending the money each month. You may quickly come to call that property a "bottomless pit." In the trade they have a name for such houses. They are called "alligators." They just keep biting at you.

## Do You Have a Landlord's Temperament?

My friend Philly decided to do just what has been described thus far in this chapter. He found that he couldn't sell his home, so he decided to rent and wait until the market got better before selling.

The property made sense, financially, as a rental. However, Philly just wasn't the sort who made a good landlord. He managed to rent the property and the first week after the tenants moved in, they called him at 11 at night to say that the sink in the master bedroom was dripping and they couldn't sleep. Could he please come over and fix it?

Those who rent property on a regular basis would have "sweet-talked" the tenants, expressing concern and suggesting they turn the water off underneath the sink, then assuring them that a plumber (or the landlord) would be out first thing in the morning.

Philly, however, had just fallen asleep when the phone rang. When he heard the problem, his response was to shout into the phone that they were disturbing his own sleep and that the tenants could damned well fix their own faucet.

At the end of the month, the tenants moved out.

Philly had to rent the place all over again. The next tenants were better. They waited until the second week to call, complaining that their furnace wouldn't go on and that it was the middle of winter and they were cold.

Philly tried to handle it better. He suggested that they build a fire in the fireplace and he'd send out a heating repair person the next day. He did and it turned out that the heat exchanger on his furnace was broken. He needed a new furnace to the tune of $1200.

He exploded. He didn't have the cash available. He told the tenants they'd have to wait until the following month when he got the money to fix the furnace.

They moved out the next day and sued him in small claims court for the half-month's rent they said they had coming. He tried to argue with the judge, but when the tenants pointed out that he refused to fix the furnace during winter, he lost.

Philly's problems were not actually financial. They were psychological. (He could have borrowed the money to fix the furnace.) He never quite understood in his mind that owning a rental property is like caring for a delicate flower. It has to be watered and pampered in order for it to prosper. Philly didn't want the bother and the headache. He wanted the rental to take care of itself. Unfortunately, that's not the way rentals are.

If you're like Philly, emotionally speaking, then you shouldn't rent out your home regardless of whether it makes financial sense. In the end you'll lose money and perhaps even ruin your health, because you'll be doing something for which you are unsuited.

On the other hand, millions of Americans rent millions of homes out each year without much hassle and much bother. And they eventually receive significant profits for doing so. It all depends on your mental attitude.

## Techniques for Handling a Rental

Sydney, a young woman living alone, found herself in the predicament of having to move to a new home, yet wanting to purchase a rental home at the same time. She had heard of the profits to be made in owning real estate (indeed, virtually all of the major fortunes made in this country involve real estate), and she wanted to be a part of it.

So, Sydney decided to rent out her present house instead of selling it. She borrowed against it (as described above) and used the money as a down payment on another house. Then she was faced with renting out her former home.

Since the house was already in good shape, she didn't have to do any fix-up work. So, she placed an ad in the local paper. It was a short three-line ad which read:

RENTAL AD
For Rent—Lovely Garden Home
3 bed, 2 bath with fireplace,
den, large garage $850 + deposit.

Sydney included her phone number and soon began receiving calls. She screened the prospective tenants to weed out those who could not afford the house or who had families too large for the property. Then she showed it.

Eventually she got several people who wanted to rent. Sydney picked up some rental application forms from a local real estate

agent and had the applicants fill them out. Then she chose the
most likely prospect for a tenant and got a credit report on the person. The credit report was terrible—the applicant never seemed to
pay bills.

So she picked the next likely candidate and got a second credit
report. This prospect had perfect credit, so she rented the property, collecting the first month's rent plus a sizable cleaning/secu-
rity deposit.

There have been, of course, maintenance problems. But Sydney
either corrected them herself or called in local work people to do
the job. In over 2 years of renting, she has had the same tenants
and hasn't had any major problems. The housing market in her
area got stronger with good price appreciation. She figures she has
made 10 percent on her money by holding the house for the extra
time, and now she plans on selling her property for a handsome
profit within the next 6 months.

All of which is to say that if you're willing to devote a little time
and energy to your rental, as well as use a bit of common sense, it's
not that hard to find and keep good tenants and to make a profit
on rental property. If you can't (or don't want to) sell your present
house when you move, converting to a rental makes excellent
sense in many circumstances. For more information on managing
a rental house, you might check into my 1995 book *The Landlord's
Trouble Shooter.*

# 13
# Controlling the Escrow

After you sign a sales agreement, either you or the agent opens an escrow account. An escrow is an independent person or corporation that might be called a stakeholder. The escrow handles your title to the property and the buyers' money and, when everything necessary to complete the transaction is in order, records the deed and gives you the money.

Today this escrow process is used in most states. However, in some states, a more informal process is occasionally used in which a real estate attorney handles all the tasks normally provided by escrow.

While custom suggests that this works, my advice is to use an independent and licensed escrow whenever possible. In most states escrows must be corporations licensed by the state and they must also carry a minimum capitalization and bonding. This gives you some protection. After all, the process of escrow involves handling all the funds for your home, sometimes hundreds of thousands of dollars. You want some assurance that the person handling these monies isn't going to take off for Acapulco with them!

## What Escrow Does

1. Prepares instructions for you and the buyers
2. Collects all documents
3. Prepares necessary documents for signatures
4. Holds all monies in a trust account
5. Handles prorations
6. Disperses monies to the appropriate parties

**139**

7. Sends the deed, trust deed, and other documents out for recording

**What Escrow Does Not Do**

1. Does not examine the property
2. Does not secure financing
3. Does not solve title problems (although the escrow officer can be very helpful in suggesting ways for you to solve title problems)
4. Does not order inspections (termite or building)
5. Does not give advice

While it should be apparent from the above list that escrow performs important functions, it also should be clear that there are other important matters that escrow does not do that must be done in order for it to close. Many of these become your responsibility as seller.

**TIP**

In most cases, the real estate agent will handle all your needs during the escrow process—after all, the agent doesn't get paid until escrow closes. However, in some cases agents can be lax, allowing important matters to slip. This can cause frustrating delays and can sometimes result in the loss of the deal.

The best way to avoid such problems is to learn what escrow requires of you for your deal to close and then stay on top of getting it. If the agent pulls all the various items together, fine. If not, be sure that you're ready to step in and take over.

## Who Controls Your Escrow?

Since most sellers usually don't handle real estate transactions on a regular basis, the agent will normally suggest a particular escrow company. The agent's choice may or may not be a wise one.

One reason is that some real estate brokerage companies own their own escrow companies (or at least they own an interest in the company). This means several things, one of which is that the agent is under pressure to get you to use the company's escrow. (Note that the agent is an independent contractor and as such cannot receive a fee for recommending a particular escrow—that might be considered a "kickback.") The problem with this is determining whether the agent is recommending a particular escrow company because it offers good services, or simply because it's in some way attached to the brokerage company.

There's yet another reason to use an independent escrow, one not owned by a real estate company, and that's the matter of control. While the essence of escrow is to be an impartial stakeholder between buyers and sellers, there are often times when the escrow has the opportunity to take or not take actions that could affect the outcome of the deal.

### Delays and Speed-ups

For example, there's the matter of time. Let's say you signed a sales agreement that calls for a 60-day escrow. You figure, naturally enough, that within two months the house will be sold and you'll need to be out. So you purchase another house and at the end of 60 days, you're all packed and ready to make the move. (Of course, you're depending on the sale of your old house in order to get the money to buy the next one.)

Only the deal doesn't close. You call the escrow officer and are told there's a short delay because the buyers' lender hasn't funded yet. It's nothing to worry about.

So you wait. Two weeks later the sellers of the house you bought are screaming at you to close their deal. If you don't close, they'll back out. But you can't close on the house you bought until you close on the house you're selling. Frantically you call the escrow officer again. You are told that the lender the buyers were using had a problem and couldn't fund, so now the buyers are finding a new lender. There's going to be at least another 30-day delay.

Thirty days! You blow your stack and call up your agent. You're between a rock and a hard place. You've got to sell your house right away or you'll lose the new home you're buying.

After a lot of hemming and hawing you finally learn that the real problem is that the buyers for your property can't qualify for a mortgage. They've been desperately scrambling from lender to lender and not one will take them. Your agent, to keep from losing the deal and the commission, has told the escrow officer to stall.

### When Information Is Withheld

What happens? If the buyer never gets a lender, you don't sell—and you can't buy and move into your new home. (Presumably you made the purchase of your new home subject to the sale of the old, so you're not out any money.)

It's a real problem that was caused in part by the escrow officer not informing you of what was really happening. When told to stall, the escrow agent simply left out important information when you called. Yes, it's true the lender wasn't funding. Yes, it's true that the lender the buyers were using had a problem. What was left out that you desperately needed to know was that you had unqualified buyers. You could have been told that weeks earlier and could have been saved a lot of frustration and problems. In addition, you might have been able to take corrective steps such as putting your house back on the market.

This is certainly not to say that all or even most agent-owned escrows operate this way. The vast majority do a capable and fine job. But I have seen problems occur. While the escrow officer is presumably neutral and never "on your side," you also don't want that person to be on somebody else's side either.

### TRAP

Some real estate agents have you sign, as part of the listing, that you agree to use their escrow company. If you don't sign, they say they won't take the listing. Call this bluff. I've never seen an agent not take a listing for a salable property because you want to use an independent escrow.

**TRAP**

Some agents may insist that you agree to their escrow company as part of the sales agreement. When you sign to sell the property you also sign to use their escrow. Refuse to sign. An agent cannot make the sale of a home contingent upon using a particular escrow company. Report an agent who tries to the state real estate regulatory agency.

## How Do I Select a Good Escrow Company?

Ideally, you ask your agent to recommend two or three different escrow companies. Then you choose. (If you don't have an agent, you'll find escrow companies listed in the yellow pages of your phone book under either Real Estate Escrow or Real Estate Title Insurance.)

In most cases, escrow companies work together with title insurance companies so that you can kill two birds with one stone—you can select both the escrow and the title insurance company at the same time.

### What to Look for When Selecting an Escrow Company

1. *Fees.* In many cases the seller pays either all or half the escrow and title insurance fees. Comparison-shop fees between different companies.

2. *Recommendations.* Ask the escrow officer for recommendations. Normally an escrow company goes through hundreds of deals a year. Surely there must one or two buyers or sellers who could recommend their services.

3. *Location.* All else being equal, get an escrow company that's located close to home. It'll save you long trips when bringing in documents.

4. *Size.* While getting a large escrow company is not a guarantee of good service, it does usually mean that there's sufficient staff to fulfill any needs that you have.

## How Does Escrow Operate?

The procedure that escrow uses can sometimes be confusing. If you understand it going in you have a lot better chance of avoiding frustration and problems.

### Step 1: Obtain Escrow Instructions

To open an escrow, you normally bring in the sales agreement. The escrow officer examines the sales agreement and then prepares two sets of instructions on the basis of that agreement: the buyers' and the sellers' sets. Essentially both sets are the same (although buyers and sellers may have to do different things as laid out in them).

The escrow instructions (also called preliminary escrow instructions) are not directions for you. They are instructions for the escrow company, telling it what to do in order to complete the deal. For example, the instructions might state that the buyer is to put in so much cash, get so much money from a new mortgage, and pay for certain fees. They might also state that you are to provide clear title, pay off the existing mortgage, and pay for certain fees such as a termite clearance.

**TIP**

Read the escrow instructions carefully. Think of them as a kind of second (and perhaps more binding) sales agreement. You'll be held to whatever's in them. I have often found errors in which the instructions differed from the sales agreement. If there's an error, get it corrected *before* you sign.

## What to Watch Out for in the Escrow Instructions

1. *Deposit.* Is it to be given to escrow? What happens to it if the buyers renege? (If it's not spelled out in the instructions, the deposit could remain in limbo in escrow indefinitely.)

2. *Down payment.* When is it to be deposited to escrow? Is it to be in the form of cash?

3. *Financing.* Is it spelled out exactly as you agreed in the sales agreement?

4. *Payoffs.* Are your loan payoffs stipulated?

5. *Prorations.* (discussed shortly): Is the date for prorating correct?

6. *Costs.* Are there any unusual or excessive costs that you have to pay?

7. *Understanding.* Do you fully understand and agree with all the escrow instructions? If not, get an explanation and, if necessary, the advice of an attorney.

## Step 2: Clear Title Problems

The second step is different for buyers than for sellers. At this juncture the buyers normally go out and seek new financing. You, however, are going to have to clear the title to your property. No problem, you say? Maybe.

Title problems crop up from the darndest places. Maybe you had a rug cleaning a couple of years ago and the cleaner did a terrible job. You refused to pay and the cleaner finally said, okay, don't worry about it.

But now, when you go to sell, you find that the cleaner put a mechanic's lien on your property for the amount of the cleaning plus costs and interest. The title company won't give clear title until the lien is removed.

Or 15 years ago you were in an auto accident. It wasn't a big deal and the other person was at fault. The insurance companies paid off and you promptly forgot about it. However, without your knowledge, the other party went to small claims court and secured a judgment against you. That judgment was filed against your property. The title company won't give clear title until that judgment is cleared.

(How can a small claims judgment be filed against you if you didn't know there was a court proceeding? In some areas of the country notice of the proceedings, which must be served to you, used to be delivered via "sewer service"—dumped in the sewer. You don't show up and the other person automatically wins. It doesn't happen often today, but if the judgment were for way back when, it could have happened.)

Or when you bought the property you needed a cosigner on the mortgage in order to qualify. You had old Uncle Charley sign. Now Uncle Charley's name is on the title to the property, only Uncle Charley died 2 years ago. The title company won't give clear title until Uncle Charley signs off.

These and other problems such as a neighbor's suit over an overreaching fruit tree or broken fence, or a zoning or building department problem with the city, or any of a dozen other items could crop up. This is not to say that they will, but they could. Normally the title company will inform the escrow officer of the problem and the officer will inform you and your agent. Now it's up to you to straighten things out.

Sometimes clearing the title problem is simple. You just pay off the mechanic's lien or the judgment. But, you say, you shouldn't have to because you don't owe the money. True, you can take it to court, spend months or even years battling and perhaps lose the sale of your home along the way. Or you can call the lien holder or judgment holder and demand that he or she sign off the lien (or you can offer to pay a quarter or half for signing off). Or you can just pay.

### TRAP

 In the past, unscrupulous individuals would place liens on properties on which they were owed nothing, usually for small amounts—a few hundred dollars. Placing a lien or other encumbrance, particularly in the form of a mortgage or trust deed, was easy. A person just went down to the county recorder's office and recorded it. (In the past, many counties required the notarization of only one name on the document for recording.)

When a homeowner went to sell, he or she discovered the lien. Since it was only a few hundred dollars, the owner usually found it easier to pay than to argue.

Today this practice generally has stopped because of the penalties against it, and because many county recorders now require the notarization of all signatures to a document. However, if you've owned your house for a long period of time, you may find one of these "clouds" on your title. Your best bet, if you do, is to have your agent confront the lien holder and demand its removal. Otherwise, you'll go to the district attorney with a complaint.

Some title problems don't involve money. Uncle Charley is dead, so it's going to be pretty tough to get his signature releasing his interest in the property. But you can go to the administrator or executor of his estate (if there is one) and get a sign-off (usually with court approval). Or you may have to contact heirs or even go to court. Hopefully, it will be a simple process. Sometimes it isn't.

Or the city or county may have put a hold on your property because you're not in compliance with some ordinance such as setback or building an addition without a permit. You probably could be forced to make corrections, but some local governments prefer just to put a hold on the title. They won't let you sell until you bring the problem in compliance. There's not much you can do in this case but comply.

### Step 3: Get All Inspections

In addition to clearing title, you must get all necessary inspections. If you haven't already done so, that may include a house and termite inspection. Normally the escrow won't order these for you. Rather, you have to contact the various companies and get the required clearances sent to escrow. (Agents will often do some of this for you.)

## Step 4: Sign Off

You sign off when everything in escrow is complete.

Normally you're not asked to sign the deed officially transmitting the property to the buyers until escrow is ready to close. Escrow is ready to close when all the conditions setting it up have been met. These include your supplying clear title, inspections, and anything else necessary, and the buyers providing the cash down payment and funding from a lender.

Normally to sign off you'll need to go down to the escrow company and sign before the escrow officer. You'll be asked to sign a deed and a few other documents, including a final escrow instructions sheet. This final sheet will show a complete breakdown of the monies from the deal and, most importantly, what you'll get. (We'll cover reasonable costs to you in the next chapter.)

### TIP

In the past, agents would often take escrow instructions out of the escrow office and bring them to your home for you to sign. If the agent was a notary public, he or she would then notarize the documents and the whole process would save you time.

In recent years, however, irregularities in notarized documents have suggested that sometimes those documents taken out of the escrow office weren't always signed by the people whose signature appeared on them. As a result, many escrow companies today require both buyers and sellers to come in and sign. (Many lenders also impose this requirement as part of getting the new mortgage.)

Once you sign, you just go home and wait. Presumably the buyers are signing their final instructions, the new mortgage, and other papers. Once escrow is complete, the escrow officer simultaneously records your deed to the buyers, the mortgage, and any other required documents. As soon as everything is recorded, a check can be issued to you.

# 14

# How to Cut Your Closing Costs

The final step in selling your home is the "closing." It is the time when you sign the deed and a few other documents, the buyers deposit their final monies into escrow, the lender funds the new loan, and the property actually trades hands. (You do not receive your check until after escrow closes.) It's also the time when you can suddenly discover a host of costs you didn't anticipate. In this chapter we'll look at the closing and how to reduce the costs to you.

## Can I Control the Costs?

Unfortunately, most of the costs that you will get as part of the closing of your transaction are going to be pretty much fixed. There won't be a great deal you can do about them. What you can watch out for is that you're not paying some of the buyers' costs or that you're not paying for some things that just weren't done or shouldn't have been done. Here's a list of typical sellers' closing costs.

### Checklist of Typical Sellers' Closing Costs

|  | YES | NO |
|---|---|---|
| 1. Commission | [ ] | [ ] |

If you've used a real estate agent and signed a listing, you can well expect to pay a commission. Just check to be sure that it's correct. Normally it's based on a percentage of the sales price. It takes only a moment to calculate it out. (Yes, escrow officers do make mathematical mistakes—and often!)

|  | YES | NO |
|---|---|---|
| 2. Taxes | [ ] | [ ] |

Normally you're required to pay your portion of taxes until the date of closing. This is called proration. Prorations are simple to understand, as long as you don't worry over them too much. There are some costs, such as taxes and insurance, which are ongoing. When a house is sold, you the seller should pay your share up until the time the title transfers, then it should be the buyer's responsibility. "Prorating" simply means determining which portion of the costs are the buyer's and which are the seller's.

In order to prorate, a date must be set upon which the prorations are based. Typically this is the close of escrow, although any other date can be used. Since you as a seller often pay taxes and insurance in advance, you can often expect to get money back from prorations. Just be sure the proration date is correct, as is the sum you're being asked to pay.

### TRAP

 Beware of any sales agreement that writes in a specific date for prorations instead of saying "close of escrow." If the deal closes early, you could end up paying a portion of the buyers' fair share of costs.

|                          | YES | NO  |
|--------------------------|-----|-----|
| 3.  Insurance            | [ ] | [ ] |

The buyers may be taking over your fire and homeowner's insurance policy. If they are, be sure that they're paying you for the unused portion. You often get money back here too.

|                          | YES | NO  |
|--------------------------|-----|-----|
| 4.  Liens and assessments | [ ] | [ ] |

You're normally expected to pay off liens and assessments before title can clear. Make sure you understand any that are here and that the dollar amounts are correct. If the buyers are assuming any of these, be sure you're not being charged a payoff.

|                                    | YES | NO  |
|------------------------------------|-----|-----|
| 5.  Title insurance/escrow charges | [ ] | [ ] |

You should have been told in advance what portion of insurance and escrow, if any, you need to pay. Normally it's done by custom in your area. For example, the sellers may pay escrow while the buyers pay title insurance, or both parties may split both costs. Be sure you're not being charged an excessive amount or the buyers' share.

## TRAP

Sometimes buyers will write in a contingency in the sales agreement that the sellers must pay for title insurance and escrow fees. If you signed such an agreement, you'll probably have to pay to close the deal. The time to argue about it is before you sign the sales agreement, not when you're ready to close escrow.

|  | YES | NO |
|---|---|---|
| 6. Inspection and other fees | [ ] | [ ] |

There are all kinds of inspection and other fees that can be charged to you. These include:

|  | YES | NO |
|---|---|---|
| Termite inspection fee | [ ] | [ ] |
| Termite removal costs | [ ] | [ ] |
| Recording deed costs | [ ] | [ ] |
| Assumption fees (if the buyers assumed your loan) | [ ] | [ ] |
| Home warranty cost | [ ] | [ ] |
| Tax service contract (if you're giving a second mortgage) | [ ] | [ ] |
| Attorney's fees | [ ] | [ ] |
| Document preparation fees | [ ] | [ ] |
| Mailing costs (if any) | [ ] | [ ] |

There may be other fees and costs as well. The question you need to ask yourself, of course, is: Are these costs necessary and reasonable? The best way to tell is to ask yourself if the cost is a surprise or not, if it's big or not.

You should know in advance what the cost for a termite inspection is. You should have agreed to the costs for removing the termites. Similarly you should have agreed to a home warranty cost and should know what it is. And if you've used an attorney, you should have discussed fees well in advance.

Most of the other costs should be minor. You shouldn't have more than $50 in recording fees. A tax service contract lets you know if the buyers don't pay their taxes and is used when you give them a second or other mortgage. The cost is usually under $25. Assumption fees, mailing costs, and other incidental fees should be very small as well.

**TRAP**

Be wary of "document preparation fees." This is a definite no-no. The escrow officer is being paid to prepare the documents. You shouldn't have to pay extra for that (unless you had a special document, such as a lease, prepared).

## What Do I Do If Final Instructions (or Costs) Are Wrong?

You've been told that escrow is ready to close and you need to go into the escrow office and sign the documents. You arrive and a pile of documents is placed before you. You begin looking over the list of costs and see that instead of a 6 percent commission, you're being charged 7 percent. Or you're being charged for all the escrow and title insurance costs instead of splitting them with the buyer. Or the arithmetic on the prorations doesn't make sense.

What should you do?

If it were me, I wouldn't sign. As soon as you sign the documents, you agree to them, errors and all. That doesn't mean that they can't be straightened out later. But it's more difficult once you've signed.

If there's a problem with the commission rate, it should be a simple matter to solve. Go back to the sales agreement. It should state exactly what the commission is.

**TIP**

I once was witness to a deal in which the sellers signed a listing for a 5 percent commission. However, the agent put in 6 percent on the sales agreement. The sellers didn't pay any attention to the commission amount on the sales agreement and didn't discover the problem until escrow was ready to close.

When confronted, the agent maintained that the sellers had agreed to the higher rate. The sellers were aghast and refused to sign. Further, they threatened to report the agent to the state licensing agency. The agent relented and took 5 percent.

The moral of this story is read and pay attention to everything you sign. Remember, your signature usually protects the other person, not you.

As a general rule, if you feel that the charges are incorrect, go back to the escrow instructions and even to the sales agreement. That is the document on which escrow is based. Ask the escrow officer to correct them.

The escrow officer is sure to protest, since correcting usually means redrawing the documents for buyer and seller. On the other hand, it's not the escrow officer's money, it's yours.

If there's a mistake in math, point it out. The escrow officer should correct it on the spot.

## Do I Need an Attorney at Closing?

Unless you're savvy enough and experienced enough to handle closing yourself, you need an attorney. If there's no problem, then obviously you don't need one. If there's a problem, then you do. Since you often need the attorney to tell if there is a problem, the answer is that it's always best to have one at the closing. It's just a good idea to have an attorney check over any documents before you sign, and real estate attorneys often will work for you throughout a transaction for a set fee, often around $500 to $1000.

### TRAP

Don't count on your agent to be there when you sign off at closing. Many agents have learned the hard way that they will automatically get blamed for anything that goes awry at closing if they are there. So they make excuses to stay away. (They're "showing property" or "presenting an offer.") You can't make your agent come to the closing, but you can make your attorney be there.

It's a good idea to ask your escrow officer for an estimate of your closing costs a week or two before escrow is scheduled to close. Since everything is computerized these days, it shouldn't take more than a few minutes to get the costs printed out. It's a lot easier to look over and analyze them in the comfort of your kitchen over a cup of coffee than under pressure in the escrow office. And you might catch a mistake or two that you'd otherwise miss.

# 15

# Special Help for Selling Condos and Co-Ops

If the home you want to sell is a condominium or a stock cooperative, you may have some special concerns. Marketing the property may involve unique problems, such as getting the approval of other owners or finding a place to hang a sign. We'll look into the special situation of selling condominiums and cooperatives in this chapter.

## Is It Harder to Sell a Condo?

Selling a condo is virtually identical to selling a single-family home in terms of the procedure followed. (A condo, after all, assures you of a "fee simple" or standard title to the property, even though you may own only the airspace within your unit.) There are, however, several problems that occur which are unique to the group-living situation of condominiums.

### A Tougher Market

It's important to understand that the market for condominiums is considerably different from the market for single-family homes. For whatever reason, condominiums, with certain exceptions, have been looked upon as somewhat less desirable than houses. As a result, for a given amount of square footage, condos have generally sold for less than single-family homes.

In addition, as soon as you put your condo on the market, you are sure to realize that the appreciation is lower as well. The general rule is that condos are the last to see price appreciation when the market goes up and the first to lose value when it goes down.

### TRAP

When you bought a condo, you generally paid less than for a detached home. (This is one of the reasons many people opt for them.) However, when you now sell you generally will receive less as well, so it may be no bargain.

### TIP

On the other hand, buyers trying to get into a high-price area may find that a condo is their only option, because of its lower price.

## When Condos Are Better

There's an important exception here, and that's for condos which have extraordinary locations. Some condominiums in downtown areas of major cities such as Manhattan, Chicago, and even parts of Los Angeles, or condos in highly desired recreation areas such as Vale and Tahoe, have seen strong appreciation and are relatively easy to sell. There are several reasons for this.

In high-density areas, condos may be the only reasonably priced private residences available. Also, since many urban condos offer guarded entrances, they may afford a degree of safety not available in private homes (a big consideration in downtown areas). In recreation areas the condo may be second home and security, and the fact that the homeowner association takes care of maintenance and repairs can be a huge plus when you want to sell.

## Tricks of Selling a Condo

In order to sell for a good price, you're going to have to find a buyer who wants the peculiar amenities that life in your condo offers. In other words, you're going to have to find a buyer much like yourself (at least as you were when you bought).

### The Sign Problem

With a single-family home, one of the best (if not the best) methods of advertising is to put a "For Sale" sign in the front yard. Since the front yard of a condo is owned by everyone in the association, you normally can't do that. Most condominium bylaws, in fact, preclude you from putting a "For Sale" sign for your condo in any common areas.

Thus letting people know that you have a condo for sale can be difficult. But not impossible.

First, use an agent. It's much harder to sell a condo FSBO than a single-family house. The agent can meet buyers at the office and then bring them by. Second, see if you can fudge on the sign. Try putting a sign in the window of your unit or on the garage door. Chances are no one will say anything about it, at least initially.

### TRAP

Some condominium homeowner associations prohibit you from even putting such a sign on the exterior walls, on doors, or in the windows of your own unit. Such rules can be hard to enforce, but strict homeowner association boards may try to.

### Advertising on Your Own

If you do try to sell FSBO, or if your agreement with your agent provides that you pay for advertising, make special arrangements for showing. Put your phone number in the ad and when buyers want to come by, arrange a time to meet them at the gate or main door to let them in.

I've used this technique myself on many occasions and it doesn't seem to bother buyers in the least. Indeed, most seem pleased to be looking at a property that has the security of a main door or locked gate.

### Talk to the HOA

The homeowner association (HOA) controls everything in a condo. But the people on the controlling board of directors are human beings too. If you have a special sign or showing problem, appeal to them. They may go out of their way to accommodate your needs.

## Is It Harder to Sell a Stock Cooperative?

With condos you get title to your property, whereas with co-ops you get stock in a corporation which entitles you to live in a unit. To sell your unit, you sell your stock.

Co-ops can have all the benefits of condos. However, co-ops in general have been limited to the East Coast and have usually been built in high-density areas. (Most condos have been built right next to single-family developments—across the country.)

Co-ops can also have all the problems involved in selling condos. They can have one additional problem that condos usually don't have. That relates to getting the approval of the other owners for your buyer.

When you sell a condo, you simply transfer title to your property via a deed, and the other owners in the condominium development may have no say whatsoever about the sale. When you sell a co-op, however, you generally transfer ownership by selling your shares of stock to the new buyers.

The procedure may involve turning your shares in to the co-op management and having it issue new shares to the buyers. Along the way, depending on how the articles of incorporation or the bylaws are written, the directors of the co-op may have some say as to whom you sell your property to. That is, they may have the right to refuse to issue stock to the new purchaser, thus effectively tying up your sale.

This control is, in fact, one of the factors that may make your co-op more valuable and desirable. Many buyers like being able to have some control over who their neighbors will be.

Of course, such control is more limited today than it was in the past. In general, co-ops may not limit buyers in terms of race, religion, or national origin. However, in recent years some exclusive co-ops have attempted to restrict buyers in terms of their income levels or their occupations.

When you go to sell, be sure you check to see what restrictions, if any, apply in your case. While you could certainly fight such restrictions, you're more likely to accomplish your goal of selling quickly if you find out the rules and then find a buyer who qualifies.

# 16

# Tax Laws
# for Sellers

If you're selling your home, you have access to some of the most generous tax advantages available to Americans. You may be able to defer the capital gain on your sale or, in certain circumstances, even have it excluded forever from your taxes. In this chapter, we'll examine the benefits home ownership offers sellers.

## Can I Avoid Paying Taxes When I Sell My Property?

Yes, you can. If the property is your main home (your principal residence), you may put off paying taxes on the capital gain you make when you sell, provided certain rules (described below) are met. In other words, if you meet all the requirements you can sell your main home, have a gain on it, move to another, and not immediately pay taxes. You "roll over" your capital gain.

It's important to understand that this works by "deferring" the tax you owe. It does not mean that the taxes are forgiven; they are only pushed off into an indefinite future. As long as you continue

---

*Note:* Over the past decade, the government has changed either the tax law or its interpretation of that law on virtually an annual basis. In addition, the tax laws as they relate to real estate have become increasingly complex. For those reasons, it is suggested that the reader use the information in this chapter as an overview of deferral and other tax procedures and leave the determination of the actual tax consequences of selling any specific property to a competent accountant or tax attorney.

---

to own your own home and meet the requirements, you do not have to pay the taxes. It's sort of like pushing a snowball uphill. It keeps getting bigger and heavier, but as long as you keep pushing, it never bowls you over.

## How Does Deferral Work?

Essentially deferral is quite easy. When you sell your house for more than you paid, you generally have capital gain (explained shortly). Normally, under today's tax structure, you would add that capital gain to your other income for the year and pay taxes on it. For example, if your gain were $20,000, you'd add that money to your income and, depending on your tax bracket, pay federal taxes (up to a maximum of 28 percent) plus state taxes. The taxes, obviously, would eat a lot out of your capital gain.

With deferral, however, you can take that gain and apply it to your next house, if you meet the rules. Instead of paying taxes immediately, you defer them into the future. You don't have to add that $20,000, in our example, to your income. You don't have to pay taxes on it in the year you sold your house.

When you sell your next house, you may be able to again defer the taxes to yet another house. There is no limit to the number of times you can defer your capital gain. You can thus keep rolling over that gain, increasing it with each home you sell. (If you die before your spouse, he or she may get a "stepped-up basis," meaning the gain, in effect, would be wiped out and there would be no tax to pay!)

Does it really work? An estimated 40 million Americans who are doing it suggests that it works very well indeed.

## What Are the Rules for "Rolling Over" a House?

Here are the rules that govern tax deferral. Please note that tax rules change constantly, as does their interpretation. Before taking any action that would have tax consequences, be sure you contact your accountant or tax attorney.

## 1. You Have 4 Years to Roll Over Your Capital Gains

This rule means that from the time you sell your current house, you have 2 years *before* or *after* (a total of 48 months) in which to purchase and move into your next home, if you want to defer the gain. If you wait too long, you could lose the deferral advantage. (Generally speaking, the rule requires that you physically occupy your new property.)

### TIP

Note that the 2-year rule means not only 2 years *after* you sell your present home but also 2 years *before* you sell it. For example, you could buy your next home and move in and then put your present home up for sale. It might take you 18 months to sell it. The deferral rule applies, since the sale and occupancy of your new home came within the 2-year period.

### TIP

There are some special exceptions if you are in the military. Check with your accountant.

The rules also apply to the building of a new home. You could sell your present home and live in an apartment for 18 months while your next house is being built. As long as your next house is completed and you are able to *move in* before 2 years have elapsed since the sale of your previous house, you can defer gain.

## 2. Deferral Applies Only to Your Principal Residence

This is a mistake that many people make. They erroneously believe that they can roll over a rental or a vacation house that they own because it is residential property.

The key is not whether it's a house, a condo, a fourplex, a town-house, or a vacation house or some other kind of residential property. The key is that it must be your main home, your *principal residence.*

You can have only one principal residence at a time. If you have two houses—one a vacation home, the other a home in the city—only one can be your principal residence. On only one can the capital gain tax be deferred.

**TIP**

The rules for what constitutes your principal residence can be quite liberal. It can be a single-family house, one-half of a duplex, one-fourth of a fourplex, a condo or time-share, or some other form of property. You might even maintain that a boat on which you live and which is permanently anchored in a harbor is your principal residence. See your accountant.

If part of your principal residence is investment property, only that part in which you live can be deferred. For example, if you own a duplex and rent out one-half, only the half in which you live is your principal residence. When you sell, half your capital gain can be deferred; the other half is taxed in the year of the sale.

### 3. There Is a 2-Year Wait Between Deferrals

You can use the deferral rule only once every 2 years. For example, you sell your principal residence and buy a second house deferring your capital gain on the sale. Within 12 months you sell that second house, purchase a third, and make a second gain. You cannot defer the capital gain on the middle property. However, if you wait 2 years between the time you sold your first house and the time you sell your third, you can defer the gain on the third.

**TIP**

There are special exceptions if you are forced to move because of a job transfer. See your accountant.

### 4. The Deferral Is Based on the Price of the New Home

In order to get the full deferral, you must buy a new home that costs more than the sales price of your old one. For example, if you sell a house for $100,000 and buy a new house for $101,000, all the capital gain on the sale of the old house can be deferred.

#### TRAP

This is tricky and has led some people to think that the *only* way you can get the deferral is to buy a more expensive home than the one you sold. This is the only way you can get the *full* deferral. You can, however, get a partial deferral even if the new house you buy costs less than the house you sold.

For example, you sell a house for $100,000 and buy another for $90,000. The new house costs $10,000 less. This means that you'll pay tax in the year of the sale on the first $10,000 of capital gain from your first house—it cannot be deferred. But any additional gain, can.

#### TIP

You can increase the tax basis (on which the deferral is made) of the home you purchase even *after* you move in by improving it, provided you make the improvements within the 2-year time limit. For example, you purchase a second home 12 months after the sale of your first home. The new home costs $110,000; the old home sold for $120,000. The new home costs $10,000 less than the old home. Presumably this $10,000 cannot be deferred.

However, within the next 6 months you add on an extra bedroom to the new home at a cost of $10,000. This addition boosts the basis for the new home to $120,000, meaning that the entire gain from the sale of your old property can be deferred.

Remember, deferring gain simply means pushing it off onto the next property and into the future. It doesn't mean that it's forgotten, forgiven, or overlooked.

## TIP

Don't think that just because you've deferred once, you have to pay taxes the next time. As long as you follow the rules (make only one sale every 2 years, stay within the other time limits, and so on), you can keep on deferring as long as you live. You can continue to defer indefinitely.

## TRAP

It's very important to understand that you cannot choose to pay taxes on your capital gain in the year it occurs. *The deferral is not optional.* If you replace your old principal residence with a new one within the time limits, you must defer the gain.

## What's the Difference Between Capital Gain and Profit?

The real confusion over gain comes when we tend to think it means profit. Profit has a much different meaning to most of us. Let's say that we purchase a house for $110,000 with a $90,000 mortgage on it. We own it for a few years and it goes up in value. We decide to take some of that equity out so we refinance and get a new first mortgage for $120,000.

A few years later we need some more money, so we take out a second mortgage for another $10,000. Now we owe $130,000 on the property.

Finally, it's time to sell and we sell for $160,000. Our costs of sale are $10,000. What's our profit?

---

### Figuring Profit on Sale

| | |
|---|---|
| Sales price | $160,000 |
| Less costs of sale | 10,000 |
| Adjusted sales price | 150,000 |
| Less mortgages | 130,000 |
| Profit | $ 20,000 |

---

For most of us, profit means the cash we get when we sell the property. In this case, the cash is $20,000. However, figuring capital gain is substantially different.

---

### Figuring Capital Gain

| | |
|---|---|
| Sales price less costs | $150,000 |
| Basis | $110,000 |
| Capital gain | $ 40,000 |

---

---

### Comparing Capital Gain with Profit

| | |
|---|---|
| Gain | $40,000 |
| Profit | $20,000 |

---

The capital gain on the sale is $40,000, while the profit is only $20,000. The reason for the discrepancy is that gain is calculated precisely using a set formula. Profit, however, is a vague concept that most homeowners use to express the equity they have in their property.

**TIP**

Refinancing does not usually affect the precise way capital gain is calculated. Refinancing, however, has everything to do with the way most people calculate their profit.

Remember in the above example that we refinanced twice, taking out cash each time. In the calculation of gain, it's not just the cash that we get when we sell that counts, but also the cash we took out while we owned the property.

## How Do I Report the Sale of My Home to the IRS?

You should report the sale of your home in the year the sale occurred on Form 2119, Sale of Your Home. If you have any taxable gain that is recognized, you should report it on Schedule D, Capital Gains and Losses.

The question arises sometimes over when you must pay tax on the gain. Generally speaking, most people who intend to replace their home choose to wait until the 2 years are up. Then, if for some reason they haven't replaced their principal residence, they go back and refile their taxes in the year of sale, paying the gain (plus any interest). On the other hand, if you don't intend to replace your principal residence, you may want to pay the tax on your capital gain in the year of sale (when you probably have the money handy).

Remember, you cannot choose not to defer paying taxes on the gain if you roll over your principal residence within the appropriate time limits.

## How Do I Calculate Capital Gain If Part of My Residence Was Used As Investment Property?

Some people rent out a portion of their home (for example, you may own a duplex). When a part of your home is your personal residence and a part is rental property, the whole matter of rollover becomes more complex.

The general rule is that you can defer tax only on the gain on that portion of your home which was exclusively your principal residence. You cannot defer paying tax on a gain on that portion which was business or investment property (rented out). Thus, the tax on that portion of the gain attributable to your principal residence can be deferred. The tax on that portion of the gain attributable to your rental, on the other hand, must be paid in the year you sold the house.

## What About the $125,000 Exclusion?

The trouble with rolling over a principal residence is that each time we roll it over, the price tends to get higher. Ultimately, when we retire, we're stuck with a very expensive house that may be too big and too costly for us to operate. What we want to do then is to cash in our house and use the money to help with retirement. But by then, we may have deferred so much capital gain that if we sell, we'll give a huge chunk to the government in taxes. Our house, in fact, may be our largest single source of wealth. What a shame to pay big taxes on our equity.

As a result of this problem, until recently many retirees were forced to keep a big house that they didn't want and couldn't afford. Or they were forced to sell and lose a substantial portion of their hoped-for retirement nest egg.

To help overcome this problem, in 1980 the government passed a special $100,000 exclusion, which was raised to $125,000 in 1981. The current $125,000 exclusion allows you to escape taxes up to that amount when you sell your home near retirement age.

What this means is that when you retire and sell your principal residence (moving to a less expensive home or even renting), up to $125,000 of the gain you had been deferring for all those years is excluded—you don't have to pay taxes on it. (*Note:* It's up to $125,000 of the gain that's excluded, not $125,000 worth of taxes.)

Here's how it works:

---

### Using the Exclusion

| | |
|---|---:|
| Sales price of your current home | $ 200,000 |
| Less exclusion | −125,000 |
| Adjusted sales price | $ 75,000 |
| Less basis of your current home | −50,000 |
| Taxable gain | $ 25,000 |

---

Notice that in this example without the exclusion you'd have to pay taxes on $150,000 worth of gain. With it you have to pay taxes only on $25,000.

Of course, you have to meet certain strict requirements to get the exclusion. However, those requirements are not difficult for most Americans who own their own principal residence and are nearing retirement age.

## What Are the Qualifying Rules for the $125,000 Exclusion?

While the exclusion rules seem simple enough on the surface, closer examination often raises some questions. Here is an overview of rules and answers to common questions regarding them. Check with your accountant for the specifics in your case.

*You must be 55 years of age on the day the sale closes (title changes hands). You may claim the exclusion only once in your lifetime.*

1. *What if we're married, but only one of us is 55 on the date of the sale and the other is younger?*   You both qualify. Only one spouse has to be 55 on the date of the sale for both to qualify. You must, however, claim the exclusion jointly.

   **TIP**

   You are considered to be 55 one day before your fifty-fifth birthday. Thus, if you turned 55 a day after your house was sold, you would still qualify.

2. *What if I claimed the exclusion once before, but now I've remarried and my wife has never claimed it? Can she claim it now?*   The answer is no. If you and your wife own the home as community property (or as tenants in common or tenants by entirety), you both must join in the choice to exclude. Since you've already excluded once before, you are barred from excluding again.

3. *Can a single person claim the exclusion?*   Certainly. In addition, you get the full exclusion, $125,000, not just half as is the case in other exclusions. Note, however, that if you marry and your spouse has not claimed the exclusion before, she cannot claim it again, as noted previously.

*The property must be your principal residence and you must have occupied it for the last 3 out of 5 years.*

4. *What if I have owned the property for only 3 years, but during that time I took a couple of vacations? I even rented it out one summer for a few weeks while I was on vacation. Since I didn't occupy the property for the full time, technically speaking, can I still qualify for the exclusion?*   Generally speaking, yes. Renting out your home for a few weeks while you were on vacation does not mean you weren't occupying for this rule.

5. *What if I took a sabbatical for a year and lived elsewhere?* Generally speaking, you could not claim that year as time during which you occupied the property. The rule seems to be that if you're away for more than a month or two you "break the chain" of occupancy.

6. *What if I owned the property for 3 out of the past 5 years, but didn't occupy it continuously? For example, for 2 years I treated it as a rental property.* The answer is that you get the exclusion as long as you occupied the property for 36 full months, regardless if that time was continuous or intermittent.

7. *What if I have been living in a condo for the past 3 out of 5 years? Does that qualify as a principal residence?* Yes. Many types of homes qualify, including stock cooperatives and mobile homes. In some cases, even yachts used as houseboats have qualified.

While these are the main rules regarding the exclusion, there are other interesting questions that arise.

8. *Can I revoke the exclusion?* Yes. For example, if you later marry and want to claim it with your new spouse, you can revoke the earlier exclusion. The time limit for this is presumably 3 years, the time you have to file an amendment to your tax return. Also, you would have to pay the taxes you didn't have to pay previously, as well as the interest.

9. *Can the exclusion be combined with deferral?* This is a most interesting question, since it suggests excellent tax planning ideas. The answer is that, in general, you can combine the exclusion with deferral of income on a principal residence. Thus you can sell your current expensive home, take out much of the cash without paying taxes on it, and then buy a smaller, less expensive home, deferring some of your equity to that next home.

**TIP**

Note that the exclusion rule does not require you to choose it when you are 55 years old. You can wait. This allows you to plan ahead and take it at the most opportune time. (Keep in mind, however, that the government both giveth and taketh away. If you choose to wait and at some time in the future the government decides to do away with the exclusion, you could lose out.)

## TRAP

Remember, the rule gives you an exclusion of *up to* $125,000. If you do not take the entire amount, you lose the difference. Thus you may want to wait until you have enough gain (deferred or otherwise) in your home to take full advantage of the exclusion.

# 17
# What to Say on a Disclosure Statement

I can remember back not so many years ago that when sellers listed their properties, the first thing they did was cover up all the problems. Holes in the foundation were spackled, cracks in walls painted over, a few new shingles placed where water leaked in, a temporary fix put on a bulging water pipe, and so on. The idea was to sell the buyers on the concept that the house was in great shape. Once buyers bought and found out otherwise, it was their problem.

Times have changed, enormously. Complaints and lawsuits by buyers against sellers (and their agents) have turned things 180 degrees around. Today savvy sellers know that if there's a problem with the house that they fail to disclose and the buyers later find out about it, the sellers might not only have to pay to have the problem corrected (usually in the most expensive way), but in an extreme case might even have to give the buyers back their money and take back the house!

Nobody wants that sort of thing to happen. When you sell your house, you want it to stay sold. And you don't want to be replacing expensive items for the buyers later on. You want a clean deal.

To get a clean deal, you must disclose what's wrong with the property. Some even argue that you must disclose what you should know is wrong with the property, even if you don't know it!

All of which is to say that today disclosure is a big part of selling. Most states today require that sellers give buyers a formal disclosure statement, and some even prescribe the basics of what goes into that statement. (Check with your agent to see what the rules are in your state.)

But even if the state doesn't tell you what you should disclose, you should prepare your own disclosure statement and give it to the buyer—if for no other reason than to protect yourself. Remember, if you tell the buyer the house has a cracked foundation and the buyer goes ahead with the purchase anyhow, what's that buyer got to complain about later on?

**TIP**

My own philosophy in selling properties that I own is to disclose everything, in great detail, no matter how small the problem appears to be. This has a big advantage in that I never have to worry about buyers coming back at me later on claiming I didn't tell them about something. It's all out in the open. If there's a problem, it's dealt with at the time of sale.

## How Far Does Disclosure Really Go?

Disclosure goes a very long way. I recently had occasion to witness a confrontation among sellers, buyers, and agent that would most certainly not have taken place 10 years ago. The situation was quite simple on the face of it.

The buyers had purchased a single-family home in what appeared to be a nice neighborhood. They had paid close to asking price and the deal went smoothly. At the closing, buyers, sellers, and agent all seemed satisfied. The deed was recorded in favor of the buyers, and the sellers received their cash out, the agent her commission.

About 2 weeks later the buyers called one of the agents (there were two agents involved in the transaction, both acting as dual agents) and complained that there was a severe problem with the home. The next-door neighbors had a teenage daughter and son. The kids would play their stereo loud during the day and then have parties two or three times a week until early in the morning. The buyers weren't able to sleep or to enjoy their property. They said they had talked to the neighbors, all to no avail.

The agent chuckled and said the kids would be kids and to ignore it. If it got really bad, they should call the cops.

A week later the agent got another phone call. The buyers had called the police, who indicated that there wasn't much they could (or were willing to) do and revealed that the former owners (the sellers) had frequently called to complain about the same thing. The buyers said they were thinking about demanding a rescission of the deal.

This caught the agent's attention. Rescission essentially means to go back in time until all the parties are where they were before the deal was made. In other words, it means to take back the sale of the property.

The agent investigated and talked to the former sellers. The neighbors had indeed been a big problem. That, it turns out, was the real reason they had decided to sell! They had filed numerous police reports against those neighbors.

"But," the agent protested, "why didn't you tell me about that? Why didn't you tell the buyers?"

"Because," came the reply, "who would have bought the house if we'd mentioned it?"

The agent suspected she was in big trouble. She went to see the neighbors, who were intransigent. They refused to curb their children.

She went to see the buyers, who had dark hollows under their eyes and who were in the process of contacting an attorney. They couldn't sleep, and if they couldn't sleep they weren't getting the "quiet enjoyment" they were entitled to from their home. The agent had to agree.

The buyers did get an attorney and did pursue the matter, although it never got to court. By then it became evident that in their state the sellers' duty to disclose defects in the house to buyers was clear. The sellers should have disclosed that there were problems with the neighbors.

How was the issue resolved? In the end, the agent negotiated with the noisy neighbors to sell their home!

It could have been much worse for the sellers. The buyers might have insisted on rescission, in which case the sellers might have had to pay back all the buyers' money and take back the house!

And it was all over noisy neighbors, something that wasn't directly a part of the house that was sold.

In recent years sellers have been held liable for a whole bundle of potential drawbacks to property that a decade ago would never have caused a raised eyebrow. These include:

A death or murder in the house being sold

A landfill nearby

Flooding, grading, or drainage problems

Zoning violations

Soil problems

Bad neighbors

And a host of other potential problems. All of which is to say that if you don't disclose any and all problems with your property, the consequences could be severe.

## It's What You *Should* Know That Counts

"But," you may be saying to yourself, "those sellers in the example lied. I would never lie. I would simply reveal everything I knew about the house."

Unfortunately, it's like getting a traffic ticket. Ignorance of the law is no excuse. It's not always what you know and disclose to the buyers that counts. It's what you should have known and should have disclosed.

Much of the disclosure precedent came from a lawsuit in California (*Easton* v. *Strassburger,* A010566, California First District Court of Appeal, February 1984). The results of this lawsuit were codified in California law and subsequently in the real estate code of many other states. The California real estate code deals primarily with agent's responsibilities and states, "An agent's duty to prospective purchasers of residential property of one to four units is: to state that he or she has conducted a reasonably competent and diligent visual inspection of the listed property and to disclose all facts revealed that materially affect the value or desirability of the property."

With regard to the sellers, the rules can be even stricter. The sellers must disclose to the buyers any defects in the property that would materially affect its value or desirability—in many cases whether or not the sellers are aware of those defects!

"But"—I'm sure many readers are frothing—"how can you disclose what you don't know?" The answer is simple. You can either conduct an inspection yourself or hire a competent inspector (discussed in the next chapter).

**TRAP**

Most of the problems with a home that a seller doesn't know anything about deal with the various systems—plumbing, heating, electrical, gas, and so on—as well as structure. You might live in a house for 10 years and be totally unaware that a problem in the gas system exists. A buyer could purchase the home and it might blow up the next week. It could be argued that you should have had an inspection of the gas system to protect the buyer.

## Am I Warranting the House When I Disclose a Problem?

While you must disclose problems and defects in your home, you don't necessarily have to fix them, unless they are a safety hazard. For example, your lot could have a perennial drainage problem. Every winter the storms in the nearby hills drop several inches of rain that floods your backyard. The flooding lasts for about a week and then drains away. The buyers could be made *fully aware* of the problem and still purchase the house with the existing condition.

Or you could be near a landfill that occasionally produces noxious smells. As long as the buyer is made fully aware of the problem and agrees to buy the house with it, you're probably okay. (What, for example, could you do about the landfill?)

Of course, deciding on the difference between what must be fixed and what might not be done could be the job of a Solomon. However, one thing is clear. The more you disclose to a buyer, the less chance there is for you to have trouble later on.

**TRAP**

Some sellers and their agents have taken to selling homes on an "as is" basis in the hopes of getting around the disclosure dilemma. This simply does not work. Asking buyers to take a property "as is" does not negate the need to disclose problems. Oh, you *can* ask the buyers to take the house "as is," but only after you've disclosed all the problems and the buyers know what they are getting.

## When Should I Disclose Problems?

The sooner the better. It's important to understand that to avoid any possibility of problems, you should disclose defects or problems with your house as soon as possible. That means even *before* the buyer makes an offer. In other words, if you're using an agent, the agent should present your disclosure sheet to the buyer before accepting an offer. If you're handling the house yourself, you could present it to the buyer before accepting any money or signing any sales agreement.

### TIP

The idea is that the more you get out on the table before the sale, the less you have to worry about afterward.

Be sure that the disclosure sheet is made at least in duplicate and that you retain a copy signed by the buyers stating that they have seen and had a chance to read it.

### TRAP

If you hold off showing the disclosure sheet until after the buyer makes an offer you accept, the buyer may have the right to take back the offer, once the disclosure is given.

## What About Buyers Who Balk at a Problem?

The downside of disclosing is that it may cause a buyer to refuse to make an offer. Or to make a much lower offer.

The solution here is to confront the problem out in the open and deal with it. There are two ways to do this: You can either fix the problem, or give the buyers a cash discount because of it.

The most common example I know of has to do with leaky roofs. You, the seller, disclose that your roof leaks. The buyers don't want to buy a house with a leaky roof.

You can do one of two things. Before you put the house on the market, fix the roof. If the roof is basically in good shape, but just has a few leaks, it won't be that expensive. Then, you can disclose both that the roof used to have leaks, but that you had it fixed.

Or, if the roof is in terrible shape and must be replaced, you offer the buyers a discount or replace the roof yourself. I like the discount idea here because there are many kinds of roofs and the buyers may want a more expensive (or less expensive) roof than you would choose.

### TRAP

If you disclose a bad roof and offer a discount to the buyers, the lender may require that the roof be replaced before funding. If this is the case, you may have no choice but to go ahead and replace it yourself. But at least consult with the buyers so you don't put something on that they hate and that will cause them to back out of the deal.

To help sellers with their disclosures, agents and some real estate associations have created their own disclosure sheet forms. (If you're not using an agent, you can usually get a copy from an agent.) These are given to prospective buyers and they help the sellers organize their disclosures. Here's what a typical disclosure statement might contain. (*Note:* Check with an agent/attorney to see if a more specific disclosure statement is required in your area.)

## Typical Disclosure Statement

*Occupancy:* Who is occupying the property? If it's a tenant, will there be any difficulties in getting possession?

*Appliances and features contained on the property* (note that the following is only a partial checklist:)

| | |
|---|---|
| Oven | Trash compactor |
| Range | Microwave |
| Dishwasher | Washer/dryer hookups |
| Sewer | Septic tank |
| TV antenna | Security system |
| Well | Wall air conditioners |
| Sprinklers | Solar heating |
| Gutters | Fire alarm |
| Intercom | Gazebo |
| Spa | Carport |
| Garage | Garage door opener |
| Pool | Heater/filter |
| Window screens | Satellite dish |
| Exhaust fan | Garbage disposal |
| Fireplace | 220-volt wiring |

*Roof:* Age, type, and condition

*Defects or problem areas in the house:*

| | |
|---|---|
| Interior walls | Exterior walls |
| Ceilings | Floors |
| Roof | Insulation |
| Windows | Doors |
| Foundation | Slab |
| Driveway | Sidewalk |
| Fences | Gates |
| Electrical | Plumbing |
| Sewer | Heating/cooling |
| Structure | |

*Other problem areas:*

1. Is there a homeowner association?
2. Are there any common areas? Describe them.
3. Are there any lawsuits which might affect the property?
4. Any deed restrictions or other CC&R restrictions?

5. Any bond obligations (such as a bond to pay for a sewer connection)?

6. Any zoning or setback violations?

7. Any damage to the property from fires?

8. Any damage from flooding or earthquakes?

9. Any settling or soil slippage?

10. Any room additions made without a building permit?

11. Any encroachments from neighboring properties?

12. Any easements?

13. Any landfill on the property?

14. Any common fences or driveways shared with neighbors?

15. Any other problems with the property?

# 18

# Inspecting Your Home

Do you need a home inspection when you sell?

If you have any doubt about that, reread the last chapter. The home inspection, presumably, protects the buyers by revealing any hidden problems. What it does even more than that, however, is help protect you by showing you've made a serious effort to discover any problems that might exist in your home. When the buyers ask you to pay for a home inspection, don't flinch. Do it. If the buyers don't mention it, either get them to sign that they specifically decline to have the home inspected and release you from any hidden defects, or do it on your own and give a copy of the report to the buyers (and get their signatures on it).

Given that an inspection is necessary, how do you go about getting one? Rest assured, it's not hard. But it can be tricky.

The answer that many sellers are using these days is the home inspector. The inspector solves a whole series of problems. If the inspector you use is bonded and a problem arises after the sale, it is easy enough to say to the buyers, "I didn't know there was a problem. I had the house inspected and I trusted the word of the inspector. Blame the inspector!"

That, of course, doesn't get you off the hook, but it does help things. In addition, if there are damages to be paid and the inspector is to blame and is bonded, the inspector may have to pay them instead of you.

Thus, using an inspector can be very worthwhile.

### TRAP

Most inspectors are gun-shy these days. They are wary of missing something and having buyers or sellers come back at them later. As a consequence, they fill their report

**183**

with so many disclaimers (and sometimes do such a cursory job) that the report is virtually useless.

## Where Do I Find an Inspector?

These days most inspectors advertise in the yellow pages and in newspapers. However, be aware that as of this writing, inspectors are not yet licensed in most states. Anyone can be an inspector—you, I, or the woman next door. Therefore, pick your inspector carefully.

Ask for recommendations from agents. Most agents know one or two inspectors whom they rely upon and trust.

Ask the inspector you're considering for a couple of references. Then call these people. Chances are the inspection was made a few months ago and they've already moved in. Did they find that the inspector missed anything? Were they otherwise satisfied?

I like an inspector who has a general knowledge plus a degree in one or more property-related fields, such as soils engineering. Retired city building and safety department inspectors are often good choices.

Recently contractors, particularly those who haven't had a terrific year, have taken to house inspections as a way of raising additional money. (A house inspection typically costs between $250 and $350 as of this writing.) A contractor can walk through your house, put checks on a form, and pick up several hundred dollars for a few hour's work. Also, if there's a problem, the contractor can then recommend his or her own company for the repair work. It's not surprising that many are doing so.

But are contractors qualified? Some are and some aren't. A contractor who builds houses new may not know a great deal about old houses. A plumbing contractor may not know about electrical. A cement contractor may know very little about roofs. The value of their inspections may be questionable.

One way of qualifying a potential house inspector is to insist that he or she be a member of ASHI (American Society of Home Inspectors) or NAHI (National Association of Home Inspectors). These are trade organizations which have been endeavoring to raise the standards of house inspectors in general.

## What Should I Inspect?

There are many areas of the home that sellers should be aware of and that should be inspected either by you or by a competent inspector. These include, but are not limited to, the following:

1. Fireplace and fireplace exhaust: Loose bricks, blockage, chimney lining.

2. Electrical system: Circuit breakers, wall receptacles, switches, wiring, light fixtures, adequacy of grounding.

3. Heating/cooling system: Combustion chamber, cleanliness of heater, blockages, compression in air conditioners, motors.

4. Plumbing: Type of pipe and age, rusting, leaks, water disposal condition, water pressure (too high or too low).

5. Sewerage, septic tank, and other waste disposal: Leakage, breakage, blockage.

6. Foundation and structure: Cracks, breaks, leaning, flooding in basement.

7. Additions made without building department approval: Room additions, window or door changes.

8. Exterior and roof: Age of exterior and roof and condition, gutters and downspouts, cracking of stucco, peeling of paint.

9. Doors and windows (including leakage): Weather stripping, hinges, alignment.

10. Drainage and flooding: Slope, groundwater conditions, drainage away from house.

11. Interior: Condition of walls, ceilings, carpets, and drapes.

12. Lot: Safety of fences and gates, any obstructions.

13. Appliances: Age and condition.

### TRAP

Beware of contractors who offer to do a home inspection for a nominal fee, then find something wrong and offer to fix it, usually for a high fee. Some unscrupulous contractors have been using home inspection as a way of procuring business. A good rule of thumb is not to have the person do the work who does the inspection. (Also, don't ask the inspector to refer you to someone. That someone could be the inspector's brother-in-law or sister, who is in on the scam.)

**TIP**

It should go without saying that you should always insist on a written report. However, in truth, accompanying the inspector on the inspection, asking questions, and getting oral answers may prove the most useful of all.

## Should I Have a Termite Inspection?

Termite inspections are not really a new part of the home inspection process. Lenders have been requiring termite inspections as a condition for approving a new home loan for decades. A termite inspection and the repair of damage have been requirements of home sales for almost as long a time. In almost all states termite inspectors are licensed, and their written reports must be registered. Usually the seller pays for the termite inspection and for correction of any damages. The buyer usually pays to have any preventive work.

## Should I Get a Home Warranty?

In addition to an inspection, you can obtain a home warranty which covers the major systems (heating, electrical, plumbing) as well as appliances. The home warranty usually costs about $300 a year (with the seller paying the first year) and may be money well spent. If minor (and sometimes major) problems crop up, the warranty often covers them, instead of you. Contact an agent for home warranty companies available in your area.

# 19

# What to Do When It Just Won't Sell

Do you have a problem house? You put the home up for sale, and for whatever reason the property doesn't sell. And doesn't sell. And still doesn't sell.

This can be one of life's more frustrating situations. It can lead to indigestion, difficulties at work, and even marital problems.

A lot of the frustration associated with problem houses has to do with anticipation. You decide to list (or to sell FSBO) and look forward to a sale within a "reasonable" time. What's reasonable? For most people it's anywhere within a month or two or three. If it takes longer, fears begin to creep in that maybe the house won't sell, ever. Maybe there's something wrong with it. Maybe you can't get the price you need. Maybe...

There are a lot of maybes possible and when you have anticipated that your home is going to sell and it doesn't, they all come to mind.

## What Should I Do?

The first thing that you as a seller should do when your house doesn't sell as fast as you hoped it would is to dump those fears that you have. Yes, you can sell your house. For every home, there is a buyer. You just haven't found yours yet. Ultimately, there is no house that can't be sold, unless the market is dead. If other houses are selling, yours can be sold too.

What you have to do is to stand back and analyze the situation. Find out what's causing the problem and take steps to correct it. That's what we're going to do in this chapter.

## Why Isn't My House Selling?

Generally you can trace the problem back to one or more of seven reasons that we've covered at various places in this book. If your house isn't selling, the reason(s) is below:

1. *Time.* You just haven't given it enough time.

2. *Exposure.* Not enough people know it's for sale.

3. *Market.* Sales are very slow.

4. *Neighborhood.* The neighborhood's real bad, so you must work on other areas.

5. *Condition.* You haven't fixed it up enough.

6. *Price.* You're asking above-market price.

7. *Terms.* You aren't competing effectively with other sellers.

While many of these reasons for not selling are related, for simplicity we'll consider each separately.

## Have I Given It Enough Time?

Perhaps, not realistically. Remember that the amount of time that it takes to sell a home differs with each property. Perhaps you went to a local agent and discovered that the average time to sell a home in your area was 75 days. So, you assumed your home would sell within 2 months. Now 3 months have gone by and it hasn't sold. What happened?

Perhaps something is indeed wrong and you should check out the other causes for not selling listed below. But, assuming that one or more of those aren't amiss, perhaps you just have to give it more time. Remember, to sell a house you need only one buyer. But, like fishing, you have to wait for that buyer to get hooked.

**TIP**

The newer the listing, the easier it is to sell at full price. The longer you have your home on the market, the more you'll have to drop your price to attract buyers.

**TRAP**

The average length of time for sale is just that, an "average." Remember, just as many houses take longer to sell as sell quicker. In some areas of the country it takes longer, 180 days or more.

## Has the Word Spread About My House?

Lack of exposure simply means that enough buyers haven't been made aware of the fact that your home is for sale. There are several ways of tracking exposure.

1. *Count the number of buyers who come through your house.* Counting heads is the easiest approach. Or you can have a little sign-in book at the door. If you haven't had a visit from a buyer in several weeks, it's a bad sign. On the other hand, if buyers keep coming through and looking and there are no offers, you may have a problem with price or terms.

2. *Count the number of real estate people who come through.* Assuming you have your house listed, you should have "caravans" of agents coming through, particularly when the house first goes on the market. Whole offices of agents, who are now aware your property is listed, will come by to see it, to remember it, and to determine if they have any buyers for it. Later, individual agents will come by seeing if your house is right for a particular buyer they have.

When agents come by, they usually leave their business card. Count the cards. If there are only a few, it could mean trouble. Agents know that they can't see all the houses for sale; thus, they pick out only the most likely ones. Few business cards means they may be avoiding your house. Call your agent and ask if she has been "talking up" your house at agents' meetings. Ask if there is something you can do, such as offering a bonus to the selling agent, that will spark interest.

3. *Count the number of calls that you get.* If you're selling FSBO, you undoubtedly have a sign out and an ad in the paper. If you do, you're bound to get calls. If those calls don't come in or if there are

very few of them, or if the potential buyers who call are confused about what you're selling or hang up when you explain what you've got, you may have a problem. Recheck your advertising for clarity and impact. Make sure *you* call back everyone who rings you up.

## Is the Market Off?

Have you analyzed the local real estate market to see what condition it's in? You can expect a sale in a reasonable time in a hot or stable market. But if the market's declining or in recession, it may take a very long time to sell.

If your reanalyze the market and are convinced that it's strong, then look closely at other factors, particularly the condition of your home, the neighborhood, and the price.

On the other hand, if you discover that the market is weak, then some reevaluation regarding the sale may be in order. In a cold market you may not be able to sell your home for a reasonable price, regardless of how much time you spend trying, until the market turns around. In a very bad market, there simply aren't any buyers at all.

### What Can I Do in a Weak Market to Help Get a Sale?

1. *Offer creative financing.* (Reread Chapter 10.) Carry back paper instead of insisting on cash. You can double or triple the number of potential buyers in this way.

2. *Rent your house.* (Reread Chapter 12.) The good thing about bad markets is that they don't last forever. While it may be impossible to sell for what you have put into your house, you may be able to rent it quite easily. (Of course, this assumes that you're moving.) Even if you have to rent it for just your payments—even for a little less than your payments—you could then hang onto it and get through the rough times.

If you need the money from your home to purchase another, borrow it. If you have good credit, a lender should be more than willing to loan you most of your equity, and you can pay back the loan with the rent.

Eventually the market will turn around and when it does, you can then put your home up for sale, successfully.

3. *Offer a lease option.* (Reread Chapter 11.) With a lease option, you in effect rent your house except that the tenant has the option to buy it at a later date for a set price.

Many would-be buyers who don't have much cash or credit are looking for lease options. Typically under a lease option the tenant pays more than market rent each month, and after a set period of time a portion of the rent is applied toward the down payment.

Lease options will often attract people and get your house rented/sold in a very cold market.

## What If I've Got a Terrible Neighborhood?

Everyone knows that the three biggest considerations when buying real estate are location, location, and location. However, you may think that your neighborhood is okay, only to realize that others don't feel the same way. For example, your neighborhood may have deteriorated during the time you've lived there and you haven't really noticed. Or a big lumber mill a mile away never bothered you, but it turns off potential buyers.

You'll know if the neighborhood is the problem because people will tell you. Agents will tell you. Home hunters who stop by will tell you (if you ask). Even some of your neighbors will tell you.

If it turns out that your house isn't selling because it's in a bad location, what can you do about it? The best thing you could have done was to have bought in a better neighborhood. (Remember this for next time.) However, since you have already bought in, the one thing you cannot do is to change your home's location. If there's a landfill nearby or a swampy river or a blighted area, you can't move your house somewhere else. You can, however, endeavor within certain limits to change the neighborhood. People who wanted to sell their homes but were unable to eventually got the Love Canal cleaned up. In Southern California in several instances homeowners got landfill dumps closed. In other cases, sellers have created local homeowner associations which have made efforts to clean up neighborhoods.

All these things take time and effort. However, if you're willing, they can ultimately produce results for you in the form of a sale.

You can also do other things, such as lowering the price. A good comparison here is the case of automobiles in a used-car lot. You walk in and, of course, look at all the shiny models. But your wallet is a bit slim that day and you ask the dealer if there might not be a less expensive car available.

The dealer leads you to the back of the lot, where there are a row of cars in not-so-hot condition, at least appearance-wise. The dealer says they all run great, but they need a coat of paint. However, to compensate for their appearance, the dealer will knock down the price 10 percent and carry the financing.

Would you buy?

Many people will. Many people will buy in a worse neighborhood if they can get a better deal. In some cases they need the better deal in order to buy at all. In other cases they just like to get good deals. When the neighborhood is bad, lower the price and offer better terms. Do it gradually until you reach a point where you find a buyer who's interested.

### TRAP

When you go to buy a new house after you sell, don't look for these kinds of "deals" in undesirable neighborhoods. No matter how much lower the price or how much better the terms, location must remain your number-one consideration. Buy for less because of neighborhood and later on you'll have to sell for less (and it will take longer). In addition, price appreciation is always slower in the less desirable neighborhoods. Finally, if you make the mistake of buying in an undesirable neighborhood, you'll have the same problems as now when you go to resell later on down the road.

## But What If My House Is in Terrible Condition?

You know the answer—fix it up!

In Chapters 1 and 8 we dealt with condition. Maybe you read

them and felt that your home was in good enough condition. But it hasn't sold and you're beginning to wonder. Now's the time to get an educated second opinion.

Call in your agent (or ask others who come by) how your house compares in condition with similar homes on the market. Be aware that most people will hesitate to come right out and say that your place is a dog, out of a desire not to offend you. But nearly everyone will drop hints. "Your house is lovely, except for that swamp of a pool in the backyard." Or, "No problems, except the carpeting has all those spots." Or, "It looks great and will look even better once you get a new roof on." Or, "Nothing wrong with it that a new coat of paint won't fix."

Take these comments to heart. Very often others see the true condition of your property far clearer than you, the owner, do. As sellers, we tend to overlook the bad and exaggerate the good. Potential buyers are not nearly so generous.

**TIP**

Remember to work on the "curb appeal" of your home. Real estate agents recognize it as a fact of life that when dealing with buyers "first impressions count most." If your house looks beautiful when potential buyers drive up and first see it, those buyers are going to be favorably inclined toward the house, even if it's not perfect on the inside. This is called "curb appeal." Make it work for you, not against you.

One of the things you can do is to drive by your home with friends or neighbors in the car and ask them what they initially see about your house that they like and don't like. Agents can also provide good clues here. Then take corrective measures.

If your house isn't selling because of some problem with its condition, take heart. You're far better off than the poor soul whose house won't sell because of location. You can't change location, but you can change condition. Often minor cosmetic changes such as paint, new lawn, and shrubs can make a world of difference.

Discover the problem and correct it, and you should be well on the way toward selling that house.

## But What If I Don't Want to Lower My Price?

What if the sole reason your house isn't selling is the price?

You've checked the neighborhood and condition and everything else and there's no problem there. It's just that those ornery buyers don't want to pay what your house is worth.

Maybe it's not worth what you think.

But you may not want to lower your price. You may have calculated what you have put into the house and what you want to get out and, by gosh, you're not settling for a penny less!

If that's the case, then don't. The general rule in real estate is that you can sell any property for any price, *if you wait long enough.*

It's largely a function of time and inflation. A seller's asking $100,000 for his property, but agents tell him it's not worth more than $90,000. He tells the agents to take a flying leap and keeps his property for sale and on the market.

Five years later a buyer walks in and offers him $98,000 cash. That's close enough, he says, and takes it. Has he shown all the naysayers?

Hardly.

Enough time passed and inflation moved up far enough so that both finally caught up with his price. However, the seller could have sold sooner for less and moved into another house. Further, if he chose the next house more wisely, it might have appreciated and earned him far more than the extra $8000 he finally received.

Most important of all, the seller could have gotten on with his life, instead being stuck trying to sell a home for years.

**TIP**

Sometimes it's better to just bite the bullet, take your loss, and move on. That way you've got every chance of making the loss back and more on future deals.

The moral to this story is that it's no good being stubborn about price. The more stubborn you are, the more likely you're going to hurt yourself.

## Should I Offer Better Terms?

Terms are the area of a real estate transaction where there is the most confusion. It's also the area of greatest opportunity.

### TIP

Almost all buyers (and sellers) are hung up on price. Almost no buyers understand yield or terms. If you're willing to let the buyer have his or her price, you can often cut a deal that is so favorable to you in terms that it's better than getting your price!

Many times price isn't the problem it seems to be. The real problem, for example, could be high interest rates. It has been estimated that each time the mortgage interest rate goes up 1 percent, another 15 to 20 percent of potential buyers are forced out of the market—they just can't make the payments on the mortgages they need to buy.

If you're trying to sell when interest rates are rising, offer better terms. Chances are that there are plenty of buyers just dying to purchase, but they can't because they can't afford (can't qualify for) the higher payments that higher interest rates produce. You can offer such buyers lower payments.

How you do this depends on your current financing. If you have an assumable FHA or VA loan on the property, you can allow the buyer to take over your own low payments.

Most people, however, are not in that type of fortunate position. Most people have a "conventional" (nongovernment guaranteed or insured) nonassumable loan on their property. The new buyers are going to have to get a new loan. But that doesn't mean that you can't still offer favorable terms. Depending on your equity, you can offer a second mortgage with reduced payments. (See Chapter 10.)

If you find a great buyer with strong credit, offer a "no pay-ments" second. (All the money including interest is due in 3 years.) That will significantly reduce the buyer's overall payments (first mortgage and second combined).

Would a buyer go for such a deal? Many buyers would be thrilled. There would be no payments on the second for 3 years and, hopefully, by then interest rates would have dropped and the buyer could refinance, paying off the second with a larger, lower-interest-rate first.

Or maybe interest rates and mortgage payments aren't the problem. Depending on the buyer's needs, you may want to provide more favorable terms in other areas. For example, you may want to modify your occupancy demands to allow a buyer to get in sooner or later. You could offer to rent back the property for 6 months to help a buyer.

All of which is to say that if it won't sell, consider improving the terms you're offering. Sweetening the pot here may get you a quicker sale and your price.

### Suggestions for a Difficult-to-Sell Property

1. Give it more time.
2. Get a new agent.
3. Advertise more heavily.
4. Offer creative financing.
5. Rent out your house.
6. Offer a lease option.
7. Start a neighborhood improvement group.
8. Get city or county help in cleaning up your neighborhood.
9. Start petitions to close landfills, obnoxious plants, and other neighborhood detractions.
10. Paint your house.
11. Fix up your yard.
12. Improve the curb appeal of your house.
13. Lower your price.
14. Carry back a second mortgage.
15. Offer a "no payment" mortgage.

# Index

## About the Author

Robert Irwin has been a successful real estate broker for more than 30 years, helping buyers and sellers alike through every kind of real estate transaction. He also serves as a consultant to lenders, investors, and brokers. Irwin is one of the most knowledgeable and prolific writers in the real estate field, with such books to his credit as *Tips & Traps When Buying a Home*; *Tips & Traps When Mortgage Hunting*; *Tips & Traps for Making Money in Real Estate*; *Tips & Traps for Saving on All Your Real Estate Taxes*; *Buy, Rent & Hold; How to Find Hidden Real Estate Bargains;* and *The McGraw-Hill Real Estate Handbook.* Robert Irwin is based in Los Angeles, California.